MONASTIC WISDOM SERIES: NUMBER THIRTY-THREE

Cristiana Piccardo, OCSO

Living Wisdom

*The Mission
and Transmission
of Monasticism*

MONASTIC WISDOM SERIES: NUMBER THIRTY-THREE

Living Wisdom

The Mission and Transmission of Monasticism

Cristiana Piccardo, OCSO

Translated by

Erik Varden, OCSO

α

Cistercian Publications
www.cistercianpublications.org

LITURGICAL PRESS
Collegeville, Minnesota
www.litpress.org

A Cistercian Publications title published by Liturgical Press

Cistercian Publications
Editorial Offices
161 Grosvenor Street
Athens, Ohio 45701
www.cistercianpublications.org

This title was originally published in Italian as *Pedagogia Viva* © 1999 Editoriale Jaca Book S.p.A, Milano.

1   2   3   4   5   6   7   8   9

Library of Congress Cataloging-in-Publication Data

Piccardo, Cristiana.
    Living wisdom : the mission and transmission of monasticism / Cristiana Piccardo, OCSO ; translated by Erik Varden, OCSO.
        pages cm. — (Monastic wisdom series ; no. 33)
    ISBN 978-0-87907-033-5 — ISBN 978-0-87907-696-2 (ebook)
    1. Trappists.   2. Cistercians.   3. Monasticism and religious orders.
4. Monastic and religious life.   I. Title.

BX4102.3.P5313   2013
255'.12—dc23   2013019482

CONTENTS

PREFACE

The vitality of Christian life is the work of the Spirit in the hearts of human beings drawn together into communities of faith and bearing witness to the living power of Christ by their faith, hope, and love. This witness has an inner or inter-subjective dimension of communion, but it also reaches out in mission, in order to meet all men and women, to accompany them on their journey, and to share with them the experience of the Risen Lord. It is a profoundly personal and utterly human experience, and, in that sense, it is a matter of individual stories and particular circumstances. It is not in the end about policies, strategies, or generalities. This is, at bottom, how the Gospel is preached to the ends of the earth.

Cristiana Piccardo tells such a story in this book, translated by Erik Varden, a fellow Cistercian monk, who knows her monastic community well. Mother Cristiana was born in Genova, Italy, in 1925, and in 1958 she entered a monastery of Trappistine Cistercian nuns not far to the north of Rome, at Vitorchiano. In 1964 she became the abbess and, under her care, the community undertook an extraordinary series of five monastic foundations around the world. She left Vitorchiano herself to be the superior of their Venezuelan foundation from 1991 to 2002. She still lives there, although she continues to travel and give conferences around the world. This book is a witness to her vision of the vibrancy of monastic life at the heart of the Church.

The monastery of Vitorchiano itself has a story to tell. In 1875, a group of French nuns, under Mother Thérèse Astoin, founded the first Trappistine house in Italy near Turin at San

Vito in difficult circumstances, such that they had to transfer
in 1898 to Grottaferrata, near Rome, where the community
continued bravely to struggle with great hardship. Finally, in
1957, the community transferred to Vitorchiano, on the out-
skirts of Viterbo, to the north of Rome. Here at last it found
fertile soil in which to bear the rich harvest which is the basis
of the reflections in this book.

The community currently numbers about seventy-five nuns
of all ages and at all stages of monastic life. It is an inspiration to anyone who has any doubts about monasticism in the
Church today. Their contemplative life of prayer, measured
by the daily round of the Liturgy of the Hours, is balanced
by the work of their hands, which includes work in the fields,
orchards and vineyards, the production of jam, printing and
cards, a life in so many ways characteristic of a thriving monastery, lived with deep humanity, wisdom, awareness of the
needs of the Church and world around them, and generosity,
both in giving and in their capacity to listen and make welcome. But what distinguishes the story that Mother Cristiana
tells is not lyricism about the enclosed life, silence, or contemplative prayer. It is her powerful *sense of the Church* and her
extraordinary conviction that mission and the transmission
of life (to use the subtitle Erik Varden has given this transla-
tion) are inherent in the nature of Christian and of monastic
community.

The reader needs to know certain special elements of the
story of Vitorchiano in order to better understand the particular vitality of the Spirit that has been so fruitful in the life
of this community. Cistercian monasticism owes much to the
sense of filiation that stems from the relationship a community has with the "motherhouse" that founded it. This gives
it a strong sense of its rootedness in a tradition of life that
has been passed on to it. Such a distinctive feature comes out
very powerfully in the way Mother Cristiana speaks about
the history of her community and her deeply appreciative
sense of the way that people have communicated a tradition of

monastic life through their own personalities in the particular circumstances in which they lived. Grace works through the "dappled beauty" of which Gerard Manley Hopkins speaks so eloquently in his poetry.

The ecclesial sense can be seen in other ways too. Mother Cristiana attributes it in a particular way to Mother Pia, abbess for many years at Grottaferrata. As a friend of Paul Couturier, she was an early promoter of ecumenism. One of the community at Grottaferrata, a Sardinian girl now known as Blessed Maria Gabriella Sagheddu (1914–1939), was profoundly taken up with this vision and offered her life for Christian unity, dying shortly after from tuberculosis. Pope John Paul II beatified her in 1983. Like Blessed Maria Gabriella, Mother Cristiana was involved with the lay movement *Azione Cattolica* in the 1950s before her entry into the monastery. Luigi Giussani (1922–2005), founder of *Comunione e Liberazione*, is an important witness in her own writing, as he has been for the community itself. These are ways in which the monastic community has come to find itself engaged in the wider dimensions of the Church's life. To understand its response to Jesus in monastic life includes a response to his call to mission.

Mother Cristiana's account of this response in the story of her community's foundations, in which she played a leading part, is a remarkable story in contemporary monasticism, especially in the history of the Cistercian Order. Her reflections on the Church and on community life that are the fruit of her experience of this story are no less an impressive contribution to contemporary monastic theology, especially as it comes with the authenticity of thinking "with its feet on the ground" rather than too much theory, though always with a fine sensitivity to the human reality which monasticism has to work with. Her appreciation of "official teaching" is instructive, as well as her sense of an obedience of faith that underlies her conviction that monastic life belongs wholly to the reality of the whole Church.

A key term for her is "pedagogy." *Pedagogia viva* is, in fact, the Italian title of the book. It is a metaphor that bears reflection.

It is easy for us to think of tradition as something passed on, a set of doctrines, a way of life, even; but we too easily think of the process as one that works through the head, by means of communication and understanding. I do not know if it is the feminine instinct at work, though certainly the role of spiritual mother plays a strong part in her understanding of filiation, but Mother Cristiana is able to show how, in the formation of her own community, far more is involved at a human level than the head. This is also borne out by the fertility of Vitorchiano's life in the story of its foundations, each as unique as any mother's children. She speaks of the real sacrifice a community makes for its fertility of life to be able to give birth, of the delicate processes of weaning the new community into autonomous life, and of the training it needs in learning to engage wholly in the new culture in which it is grounded. And all of this depends so much on the grace and gifts of the individuals concerned, who are by no means already saints!

Pedagogy is a word to treasure, then. It includes an appreciation of all the ways grace works through the life of the Church to bring us up into a living experience of Jesus Christ. It is always a fully human story, and it is a work of the Spirit that brings us (men and women) up to our full stature as one Body in Christ, to share a common sonship in the Son. For this reason, pedagogy in the Spirit engages us particularly through our participation in faith communities, of which monasteries are but one instance. This vision of ecclesiality is deeply informed by the sense of the Church that flows from the Second Vatican Council, of course, together with its strong sense of missionary vocation. I think anyone concerned for the health and future of monastic life must take to heart Mother Cristiana's reflections on how it can and must contribute to mission. The strength of her conviction here, a completely new way of thinking for me, was completely disarming.

But no less valuable for me are her honest and penetrating observations on the "inner dimension" of monastic life, the problems that need to be addressed in promoting the communion that balances the mission. It is too easy to theologize here on an abstract level that sidesteps the challenges any human community faces in terms of its affective and emotional life. Instead, Mother Cristiana talks through a number of (not exclusively) monastic issues that a community faces, regardless of the challenges of making foundations. She speaks of the need for a common vision that can unite the community at a deeper level than its shared prejudices and habits. This is particularly important when a founding community moves into new cultures, but it is a lesson she shows the Vitorchiano community lived through (patiently) in its engagement with the call to new life coming from the Second Vatican Council and the renewal movement in the Cistercian Order. She notes the challenge of educating young religious out of an inevitable initial dependence on their superiors so that they grow into adult participation in the monastic community.

This is a particular challenge where the relationships of authority and obedience are spelled out in the way the Rule of Saint Benedict states them. She talks about the importance of peer groups in formation and in a community as a whole, and the need to discover and educate the gift of leadership in a community (since foundations continually "cream it off"). Mother Cristiana's experience is wholesome and makes for a realistic discussion of what any community must deal with that is trying to live out a "spirituality of communion," which the Church calls for from monastic communities today. Mother Cristiana shows how childbirth releases new gifts of life in the mother, how sorrow is turned to joy.

This is, in the end, an extraordinary story, but one that is also a story of very ordinary people, who nevertheless have tried to let nothing stand in the way of God doing extraordinary things through them.

Dom David Foster, OSB
Downside Abbey

EDITOR'S NOTE

A few small changes have been discretely introduced by the translator into the text, all in the interest of easier comprehension by the reader of this English version of Cristiana Piccardo's book: at times very brief glosses have been added to identify a person, place, or other reference that would in all probability be unfamiliar; certain passages minimally quoted by Mother Cristiana from either books or articles have been more fully transcribed in order to provide a richer context for their relevance; and the footnotes of the original Italian now appear as endnotes.

Cistercian Publications warmly thanks Dom David Foster, OSB (Downside Abbey), for a most helpful preface that provides the reader with an indispensable frame of reference to understand the full significance of the Vitorchiano "phenomenon." And we also thank Mother Rosaria and the community of Vitorchiano for their essential assistance in helping us smooth the path for the publication of this book.

Simeon Leiva, OCSO
Editor
Monastic Wisdom Series

Introduction

The pages that follow lay no claim to being a carefully documented, academic study. They record simple conversations that have taken place within a specific community, among people who know and love one another—a simple, familiar exchange of views on an experience we have lived and suffered together. Together we have developed it in a few elements of pedagogical orientation that help us live out our fidelity to God, to the Church, to the Order, and to the House. We have sought to let remembrance emerge into the present, to let a particular past bear fruit today, to let thanksgiving for past mercies project into the future the hope that has sustained us. The pages of this book, poor as they are, are dedicated to the community of Vitorchiano, rich in its daughters, in its foundations, and in the mercy of God that, in it, overflows beyond measure.

Why, then, publish this book? Why put it before an unknown reader? Because we are certain that, within the dynamic of salvation, what has been important and precious in our small reality may have a significance that exceeds us. Because we are certain that, through the living breath of the Church, an experience entertained in a hidden spot can benefit the whole. Because we have always believed and desired that our every step, our common search (uncertain as it is), should be for the sake of the whole world. Finally, because we have thought, and continue to think, that the monastic charism is a precious talent precisely for our world of today. There are moments in history when it is good to speak about what normally remains hidden.

Monasticism and the World of Today

Today, in the wake of the so-called death of ideologies (ideologies that have always tried to answer the human heart's quest for happiness), we do not merely find ourselves facing a dearth of more or less convincing answers, or even the utopia of an answer; the questions themselves have ceased. And the loss of questions seems infinitely graver than the loss of answers. Yet there is a potential further step to be taken on the path toward oblivion. It seems worthwhile to call it to mind. In an article from *Le Monde Diplomatique* that is dated but still relevant, Eduardo Galeano, a Uruguayan thinker, speaks of the "crushing of remembrance." I wish to cite the text as it stands, for it could be important in helping us define the current face of the world:

> The culture of consumption, pressing us to purchase, condemns everything it sells to immediate obsolescence. In the twinkle of an eye things become old, to be replaced by other things, equally ephemeral. The shopping center, that temple in which we celebrate masses of consumption, is a splendid symbol of the messages that dominate our times: it stands outside time and space, it is ageless and rootless, and has no memory. Television is the supreme vehicle for disseminating such messages. It showers us with images that are born to be instantly forgotten. Each image buries the preceding one, and survives only as far as the image that succeeds it. Human events, once they have become objects of consumption, die the way things die, as soon as they have been used. Each item of news is unconnected, separated from its own past and from the past of all other events. In the era of zapping, information excess produces an excess of ignorance. Nor do the media and schools help us—that is the least we can say—to understand reality and reconstitute memory. The culture of consumption, a culture of alienation, conditions us to think that things occur because they must occur. The present moment, unable to recognize its origins, projects the future as a repetition of itself. Tomorrow is another today.

Galeano concludes:

> Memory, when it is truly alive, does not contemplate history; it incites us to make history. Memory is not to be found in museums, where it languishes, where it gets bored. It is in the air we breathe; it, in fact, breathes us. Like us, memory is contradictory. It never rests. With us, it changes. As the years go by and we change, the remembrance of things experienced, seen, and heard likewise changes. And often we lodge in memory what we wish to find there, like the police when carrying out a search warrant. Nostalgia, for example, sweetly enclosing us with its sheltering warmth, is delicious but also deceitful. Does it not happen often enough that we prefer a past we invent to a present that challenges and frightens us? But a memory that is alive does not exist to serve as an anchor. Its vocation is to be a catapult. It is not a safe haven of arrival but a point of departure. It does not disown nostalgia. But it much prefers storm-tossed hope with all its risks. The Greeks thought of memory as the daughter of time and the sea. In this they were not mistaken.[1]

In his message for the World Day of Peace in 1997, Pope John Paul II did not hesitate to affirm that "we cannot remain captives of the past. Individuals and peoples alike have need of a purification of memory."[2] For John Paul II memory signifies a consciousness of the past that confers a sense of responsibility for the present. In looking toward the future, memory is transformed into hope. But do we still possess a memory? Does the world in which we live still breathe a culture of remembrance?

It is often said that nihilism and pantheism determine all too many forms of human and social behavior in our world.[3] The perception of things as illusory, as a nothingness that does not convey any participation for human beings in ultimate Being, or again as the vague confluence of human existence in the "ocean of being" proper to pantheism, denies the authentic dimension of the human person, human individuality, and human responsibility. In some way it also denies a person's memory, for it consigns it either to the arrogance of self-invention, to a merely fragmentary perception through the impact of circumstances, or to the standardization of individuality in a dulling confusion.

In the world of today we see the sad spectacle of lives lived without any density of being, lives deprived not only of historical memory but also of that more substantial memory which is formed by the awareness of having an origin, a tradition, a destiny. Hence we have developed the tendency to adopt a radically subjective perspective on every human experience, even on religion and morals. By it, relativism of belief and ethical norms has become systematically established.

Today's world is further conditioned by the consequences of neoliberalism. In the wake of the atomic bomb that destroyed Hiroshima, the neutron bomb was born. It destroys lives while respecting material structures. Today, it would seem, we have arrived at the financial bomb, which destroys nations (and so the identity of entire peoples) by making them mere pawns in the game of globalized finance. It stands for a planetary war against humanity, against its cultural memory, its artistic and scientific diversity, its freedom to freely choose modes of production and trade, survival, and development according to the proper genius of individual peoples. The fact that global finance is becoming increasingly barbaric indicates a similar tendency in culture. It develops along the anonymously connected lines furnished so remarkably by the mass media and the explosion in information technology. Quite logically, we see the development of a mercantile mentality, a mercantile culture. Apart from the sociological consequences of such a culture (the accumulation and manipulation of wealth, the spread of poverty in increasingly vast, precarious areas ridden with unemployment, the increase of organized crime of every kind), one is struck by a cultural and, so to speak, anthropological transformation. Inevitably, a mercantile culture eliminates by way of normal practice—it is precisely the "normality" that is so terrifying—whatever it considers useless. It promotes efficiency. It banishes any gratuity of time and space to cultivate only intensive commercialization; it does not build cathedrals but giant shopping malls; it does not pause to draw breath in contemplative silence but is condensed in discotheques, in a reign of noise that banishes individuality. It does not construct memory but greedily swallows up the historical density of the past in the short-lived mood of a current fashion that will die the way it was born.

A further anguishing phenomenon worth noting is the intense compartmentalization we observe everywhere. In every sphere of our lives as individuals and as societies, procedures are increasingly marked by compartmentalized specialization. To have an illness diagnosed, we must consult a dozen different specialists; to get it cured, we must move in and out of rigorously structured sectors of help and treatment in clearly differentiated units. It is not specialization as such that is the problem but the loss of a unitary vision of life, of man, and of the world. We may obtain specific items of information, but we have lost the ability to integrate these into a wider picture of the mystery of personhood, into the unitary complexity of man, of life. Everywhere today, we observe a proliferation of religious and pseudo-religious sects. It is too reductive, clearly, to ascribe these solely to social and anthropological compartmentalization; yet it is tempting to apply the model of cultural compartmentalization, which breaks down the cohesion of social life in common, also to the religious dimension of man, to his desire for happiness and infinity, when this is channeled toward gnostic forms of expression that reduce the unitary vision of man and his destiny to limiting and partial experiences, wrapped in a haze of ritual initiation, pseudo-mystical emotions, and a metaphysics of self-affirmation.

These are but brief pointers to the contingent face of the world in which we live, the world which, tomorrow, will be diversified further still in myriad forms of expression through rapid social transformation. The perennial tradition of monasticism stands faced, today, with this reality, this challenge. We cannot avoid asking ourselves what it stands for. What on earth *is* monasticism?

Monasticism is not an attempt to proffer a response. It is not a system of belief, nor is it a specific religion. Monasticism is a vision of man and of his destiny, of being and becoming, of time and its eschatological dimension, of space projected beyond contingent limitations. This vision pours forth like a living spring from the mysteries of creation, incarnation, redemption, resurrection, and transfiguration. It is an existential vision that proceeds from faith, in faith, and is oriented toward utter faith. Monastic life emerges from humanity's constant search for the fullness of sense and significance. It is a living momentum toward happiness. It is memory that transcends time, with sights set on the eschatological fullness of the future. It is a movement of conversion, envisaging the transfiguration of our being. Monastic life takes its bearings from the incarnation and is oriented toward the incarnation. For it is in the one, infinite person of the Son of God that we find our salvation and our destiny, our beginning and our end, the fullness of life and the wellspring of all being.

In our culture of non-sense (which, with John Paul II, we may call a culture of death), monasticism manifests the positive sense of humanity and human existence. It presents itself as the space of a new humanity. Viktor Frankl, the founder of logotherapy, once declared that he had a single primary interest in life: "I have found the sense of my own life in helping others make sense of theirs."[4] His statement partly articulates the monastic phenomenon, too, inasmuch as it likewise represents a recovery of sense; or better, it is a human experience that makes sense by receiving everything it is and has from the Son of God. Monasticism carries such a radical sense of what life and destiny are for that it may offer this gift to the world as an experience of true humanity.

The wonderfully rich Cistercian tradition seems to me to be a bearer of sense in just this way. By embodying a particular wealth of humanity, a vision of man, of life, time, and space, it bestows a dimension of gratuity and beauty on human experience. It offers us a notion of relationship and life in common that freely moves within the ambit of friendship and communion as in its natural habitat. The Cistercian heritage explains conversion as progress toward transfiguration, as a "configuration" that transcends the narrow limitations of ambitious, worldly affirmation, recognizing in man an immense potential to encounter what is infinite, what is real. To a culture of non-sense, it offers sense. In this regard we may recall another interesting statement made by Viktor Frankl: "Were I to seek out the most hidden reason behind my motivation to create logotherapy, I could speak of one thing only: pity for the victims of contemporary cynicism."[5] It is impressive to see a scientist and psychiatrist denounce contemporary cynicism as the most contagious mortal illness of our times. For indeed: what better indicates the non-sense of a given period than its cynicism?

Cistercian Perspectives on Being Human, on Life, and on Time and Space

Our attempt to provide a monastic response to the predicaments of today's world is located at the level of memory, in the *recovery* of memory. It upholds the dignity and grandeur of human beings in the face of a mercantile mentality that would rob them of their sense of self. Finally, it stands for a unitary vision of man and his destiny in space and time in the face of the existential fragmentation in which we are immersed, in the face of the sectarianism and freewheeling relativism that saturates the air we all breathe.

The Cistercian Fathers provide a stupendous response to modern problems precisely at the level of anthropology. They all possess a coherent, shared understanding of human nature to which they continuously make reference. They consider man as the masterpiece of God's love, created *for* love through an overflowing of the love that is intrinsic to trinitarian life, the very essence of Godhead. Man is the masterpiece of creation, destined to participate in the infinite fullness of divine life by following a path of freedom. This path constitutes a process of transformation that is sustained by man's conscience as well as by his deepest desire. His nature is sealed by a loving positivity, a seal impressed by the creative act of God. Nothing can cancel it out, not even the inconceivable negativity of rebellion and human sin. It is this origin in love that bestows sense on human existence. It clothes man in beauty and indelible dignity.

This vision of man and of human life is thoroughly of a piece. It is unified and unifying. According to it, the very love of God has power to penetrate human beings and so to lift them out of fragmentation, out of the division caused by sin. It makes them capable, through love, of crossing the earthly, time-bound threshold of their contingency already in the here-and-now. In Baldwin of Ford, whose anthropology, for being especially accomplished and precise, holds pride of place in Cistercian patrology, we find the following statement: God did not love us "just in appearance, not just outwardly, as though it were only on the surface, but inwardly, from the bottom of his heart" (*Treatises* 13.131). This God loves us boundlessly. In the trinitarian and perfect gift of himself, he constantly leads us out of fragmentation, out of our inward and outward disorder toward the essential unity of the *form* in which we were originally created. Through the transforming embrace of his mercy, God opens up what is narrow and constricted in us.

In Baldwin of Ford these two themes go hand in hand: the human heart is enlarged, he says, when it is unified. His anthropology condenses into one our victory over fragmentation and our perfect unification in love. It is interesting to note, in Baldwin, how human beings, in distancing themselves from the love of God, are seen to be estranged from themselves, cut off from their deepest identity: "For those who roam about outside themselves and walk in [the way of] deceitful desires, those who have strayed far from their own hearts like madmen, those who are concerned with vanities and lying follies, all these are outside the wine-cellar [which is none other than the cellar of the heart]. It is they who are recalled to themselves by the Prophet when he says, 'Return, you transgressors, to your heart!'" (*Treatises* 14.145). Drawing on the biblical image of the wine-cellar, Baldwin develops a notion of interiority in spatial terms. We discover this space when we persevere within our own heart of hearts. According to Baldwin, someone who is dissipated by lust "retreats, as it were, from himself and begins to be robbed of the possession of his own land. [He begins] to be in exile within himself, just as if he were outside himself, in a strange land, in a land of forgetfulness, in the region of unlikeness" (*Treatises* 9/2.32). Only the man who recovers his roots and reclaims his humanity at the heart of the mystery of creation (where he encounters the mystery of redemption), makes the leap from forgetfulness to remembrance, from the unlikeness of fragmentation to the truth of his becoming one in the acceptance of sonship. This recovery of truth and memory affects our innermost self. It no less affects our relationships. In fact, when man utterly expels worldly affections from his heart and unifies his interior gaze, allowing himself to bathe in divine charity, his whole being becomes a place of welcome for others. It displays capacity for communion, transparency in truth, a concentration of unity in freedom. From this interior space, love of neighbor springs forth, a love that in Baldwin is tender and strong, penetrating and authentic, pregnant with memory and sense.

Monastic life leads man back to himself, to his humanity, to his heart, to his true identity. The path to follow is necessarily the path of obedience. By it, love becomes incarnate in everyday living; by it, too, we become like the Son who "learnt obedience from what he suffered" (Heb 5:8). "Charity [. . .] subjects everything to God in obedience and disposes everything by its authority: sometimes it recommends what is more perfect; sometimes it commands what is necessary; sometimes it permits what is not unlawful; sometimes it chooses what is better; and sometimes it accepts what is necessary" (*Treatises* 14.150). On account of sin, man has estranged himself from

God; this estrangement corresponds to the absence of memory. At the same time he ends up being estranged from himself. To Baldwin's way of thinking, the essential asceticism required on our path of conversion to God is just this: to overcome the estrangement of the heart, the forgetfulness of the soul. Only the heart that deliberately tends toward the full offering of itself to God becomes, once again, familiar to man. Estrangement ceases, and man returns to his own land, the land of his heart. A heart held back from this offering remains a stranger to man. Only the God-given heart can truly belong to man, as the blessed land of freedom, where he finds his true identity. When we set out, says Baldwin, our heart is not our own, we are not in our own land, for our human weakness does not permit us to love God perfectly. But never mind:

> If you cannot love as much as you should, as much as you are obliged to love, love as much as you can, as much as is in your power, as much as you are capable. [In so doing] you begin to love God here below with your whole heart— so far as it is now your own—so that in the end you may love him with your whole heart more perfectly, when [your heart], which is not yet wholly yours, is more perfectly your own. [. . .] God is a kind-hearted creditor and pours out his mercy on anyone who pays as much as he can so he may be able to pay more. (*Treatises* 3.81)

Such purification of the heart is brought about through the love of God that frees it from worldly affections. Baldwin links this process to an image of space. When he uses spatial imagery he does not merely convey an idea of breadth, order, and beauty drawn from the orientation of things and acts toward their ultimate end; nor does he intend just the image of the promised land, the land of the heart, which is at last restored to man when he recovers his sonship. In Baldwin, spatial imagery often carries a specific reference to the monastic community. It points toward perseverance in the space Providence has assigned for us, in the grace of stability and the common life. If we are faithful to the order established by God, according to the vocation he has given us, if by our obedience we give full accord to the harmony desired by the Father, we participate in the creation of a universal music, an infinite melody that Baldwin calls a "psaltery." The image reveals a fine poetic sensibility. Immense is the melodic resonance that arises from obedience and from stable perseverance in one's place in community. It is within our community that the plectrum of charity moves our hearts as individual strings on a single psaltery, creating, through our life together, an ineffable melody of mutual gift.[6]

Baldwin passes quite naturally from anthropology to ecclesiology. His vision of man—in which the love of God creates spaces of remembrance that indicate our origin and true self, in which we are set free by obedience—grants access to the promised land of life in the Church, where reciprocity of mutual giving creates a melodic consonance that already on earth expresses the canticle sung, perfectly in tune, by the angels and saints in heaven. The Church is the place of a people set free, of humanity restored to the original harmony of creation. The poet Clemente Rebora says somewhere:

When the heart soars and gives itself in love,
men invent themselves no more;
they *are*.

On this poem, Don Luigi Giussani comments as follows: "When the heart rises to the insight that everything is gift, when it makes this discovery, human beings no longer invent themselves. They cease to pretend. They no longer need to imagine what they might be. Finally they *are*. They acquire the substantial solidity which is displayed before their eyes by the stars."[7] Baldwin would add that such substantial solidity creates the infinite melody of a well-tuned psaltery, from which the plectrum draws beauty worthy of the angelic choirs. Or rather, he would say that man, at last, invents himself no longer because he discovers himself at the heart of the mystery of the Trinity. In the divine love that has indelibly sealed his humanity he encounters "the substantial solidity displayed before his eyes by the stars." The notions of "memory," "space," "unity," "dignity," "grandeur of man" flow from Baldwin's doctrine with a simplicity and immediacy that, eight centuries on, continue to amaze us, offering self-evidently prophetic answers to key questions of today.

Aelred of Rievaulx is another Cistercian Father who articulated an anthropology that is relevant, profound, and coherent. Aelred understands man as "memory, understanding, and love" (*Mirror of Charity* 1.3.9). Impressed upon the essential structure of man is a particular *form*, that is, the indelible seal of the Blessed Trinity. As in Baldwin of Ford, we are struck by Aelred's emphasis on the form's indelible character:

> By abusing free choice, then, [man] diverted his love from that changeless good and, blinded by his own self-centeredness, he directed his love to what was inferior. [. . .] Thus it very justly came about that someone who sought the likeness of God in defiance of God, the more he wanted to become similar [to God] out of curiosity, the more dissimilar he became through self-centeredness. Therefore, the image of God became disfigured in man without becoming wholly destroyed. Consequently man has memory but it is subject to forgetfulness, understanding but it is open to error, and, nonetheless, love but it is prone to self-centeredness. In this trinity within the rational soul there still persists an imprint, however faint, of the Blessed Trinity. It was stamped on the very substance of the soul. (*Mirror of Charity* 1.4.12f.)

Man drew back from God and strayed into the regions of estrangement and unlikeness. He was held captive by the darkness of human concupiscence and by the limits imposed by fragmentation. Yet the divine, trinitarian imprint was never canceled. It had been impressed forever on his very substance, with an imprint derived from the incorruptible essence of the Trinity. This anthropological vision is the source of Aelred's theology. It is likewise the source of his ideas on the ascesis of friendship, on which he constructs his doctrine of monastic conversion and of the grace of fraternal life in common. The ascesis of friendship belongs to the same trinitarian form that is impressed on the human person, for in the Blessed Trinity everything is mutual gift, mutual faithfulness, an infinite *perichoresis* and exchange of love. Aelred has a deep, striking sense of what man is. His vision embraces everything that goes into being human, including the relationships, the fraternal life in common that, to him, constitute the most concrete source of our sanctification. Indeed, Aelred does not regard friendship as a matter of the emotions but as an option of faith and reason. It calls for purification and an unconditional gift of self that must conquer every temptation to possessiveness and egoism. What is friendship? It is "to be solicitous for one another, to pray for one another, to blush for one another, to rejoice for one another, to grieve for one another's fall as one's own, to regard another's progress as one's own" (*On Spiritual Friendship* 3.101). A human relationship is a lie, Aelred seems to say, if it falls outside the sincere and heartfelt attitude of friendship toward another, toward man in general. This manner of thinking about the other, about Man in the absolute, carries a profoundly evangelical resonance. Aelred is concerned with humanizing man. Filled with the spirit of the Beatitudes, he touches on the concrete stuff of actual living: "By whatever means is in one's power, one ought to raise the weak, support the infirm, console the afflicted, restrain the wrathful" (*On Spiritual Friendship* 3.102). Such is Aelred's kind discretion that he asks his monks

> so to respect the eye of a friend as to dare to do nothing which is dishonorable, or dare to say nothing which is unbecoming. For when one fails one's friend in anything, the act ought so to well over to one's friend, that the sinner not only blushes and grieves within himself, but that even the friend who sees or hears reproaches himself as if he himself had sinned. In fact, the friend will believe that he deserves

no compassion, but that his erring companion does. (*On Spiritual Friendship* 3.102)

We recognize here the unmistakable atmosphere of the Beatitudes—the gentle face of Christ who offers himself in sacrifice and dies on the Cross as a result of taking on the sin of humankind as his own: "Father, forgive them, for they know not what they do!" (Luke 23:34). In Aelred, the altruism of friendship reaches a similar perfection. It creates a space of forgiveness in which the erring friend is not only kept from blushing and from feeling confounded on account of the fault committed; another takes his place in humble expiation, assuming the other person's sin and its consequences as his own. The ideal of humanity put before us envisages a process of substitution by which I consent to pay with my own life, reputation, or status for the freeing of another from the evil he has committed, in an ascesis of friendship that does not count the costs. In Aelred, the Christian vision of man reaches a summit. It touches the crucifying sacrifice of the most perfect altruism, of a mutual self-giving that bears abundant fruit.

We come upon comparable heights in a few contemporary saints like Maximilian Kolbe, who embodies Aelred's ideal, or Mother Teresa of Calcutta. We find it also in several unknown, uncrowned saints, such as Etty Hillesum, a young Jewish woman without explicit faith who died at Auschwitz. In her diary she wrote:

> To be true in the fullest sense of the word, to be true to God, to one's own best moments. If I have one duty in these times, it is to bear witness. [. . .] Reality is something one shoulders together with all the suffering that goes with it, and with all the difficulties. And as one shoulders them, so one's resilience grows stronger. But the *idea* of suffering [. . .] must be destroyed. And if you destroy the ideas behind which life lies imprisoned as behind bars, then you liberate your true life, its real mainsprings, and then you will also have the strength to bear real suffering, your own and the world's.[8]

We find it, too, in certain phrases of Emmanuel Mounier's when he speaks of Françoise, his young, sick daughter, who is consumed by pain:

> What sense would all this have if our little girl were nothing but ailing flesh, a suffering fragment of life, and not instead a small, white host that surpasses us all, an immensity of mystery and love that would dazzle us could we see it face to face. [. . .] We must not think of pain as of something wrenched from us, but as something that we give, in order not to be unworthy of the tiny Christ in our midst. [. . .] I do not want to lose these days. We must accept them for what they are, days full of an unknown grace.[9]

It would appear that we find ourselves, here, in a social context miles away from that presupposed by Aelred's reflections on friendship. The vision of man that emerges, however, is equally full of respect, of wonder before the grandeur of human nature. We are at the opposite extreme of the mercantile notion of man current in modern culture. Incidentally, when John Paul II addressed a million young people at Longchamp in 1997, he did not hesitate to ascertain that,

> Above all, to love is to serve. One who refuses to serve cannot be a disciple of Christ. One who does serve, meanwhile, obtains the promise of eternal salvation. [. . .] Service is the path to happiness and holiness. [. . .] The triumph, the glory of Christ reaches us through sacrifice and service. There is no greater love than that of one who gives his life for his friends—and it is not only by dying that we give our lives, we give it no less by serving. Love is the world's salvation. It builds up society and prepares us for eternity. [. . .] O young people of the world: May love and service be the founding principles of your lives![10]

In its highest magisterium, the Church thus confirms a tradition of humanity that has always flourished within the Cistercian Order. Here it constitutes, as it were, the secret sap that binds the members of a community, and the communities of

the Order, together in the law of friendship, in the imperative
of mutual giving, in the joy of mutual service, in the strength
of a profound respect that recognizes the unity of a shared
charism in the wealth of difference.

In the writings of Saint Bernard we find this dimension of
humanity indicated on every page. With limited space at my
disposal, I cannot hope to extract comprehensively from his
works that testimony of humanity I should like to bring to
the fore in response to the menacing dehumanization of our
world of today. It must suffice to cite a few statements from
his letters, letters that evidence the density and quality of
Bernard's own humanity in relationships. In them, he often
employed language that is redolent with an almost discon-
certing tenderness:

> When you wring your hands, dearest Rainald, over your
> many troubles I too am moved to tears by your affection-
> ate complaints. When you are sorrowful, I cannot but be
> sorry; nor can I hear of your troubles and worries without
> being myself worried and troubled. [. . .] As it is, I suffer
> more than enough by not having you by me, by not being
> able to see anything of you and enjoy the comfort of your
> company, so that I am at times tempted to regret having sent
> you away. True, it was at the behest of charity that I did so,
> yet whatever the need might have been, because I cannot
> see you, I mourn for you as lost to me.[11]

See also his famous letter to William of Saint-Thierry:

> O Lord, who searchest the hearts of men! O Sun of Justice,
> whose rays enlighten the hearts of men with diverse graces!
> Thou knowest and I feel that by thy gift I love this man for
> the sake of his goodness. But how much I love him, that I
> cannot tell, thou knowest. It is Thou, Lord, who givest the
> power to love, and it is thou who knowest how much thou
> hast given him to love me and me to love him.[12]

On the one hand, such a wealth of humanity rests on Bernard's
acute insight that all things are drawn toward the presence of

God; that human relationships, friendship, and mutual giving
simply manifest and pass on the intimate essence of trinitarian love, as signs of the Lord's presence among humankind
and of a constant loving conversation between the individual
soul and God. On the other hand, the rich humanity of Bernard arose out of great freedom, springing from the truth he
sought tirelessly. This hunger for truth made him forthright
in roundly rebuking sin even in sinners he held very dear:

> You foolish boy! Who has bewitched you to break the vows
> which adorned your lips? [. . .] I have said this, my son,
> not to put you to shame, but to help you as a loving father
> because you have many masters in Christ, yet you have few
> fathers. [. . .] Sadly I weep, not for my lost labor, but for the
> unhappy state of my lost child. Do you prefer that another
> should rejoice in you who has not labored for you? My case
> is the same as that of the harlot Solomon judged, whose
> child was stealthily taken by another who had overlain and
> killed her own. You too were taken from my side, cut from
> me. My heart cannot forget you, half of it went with you,
> and what remains cannot but suffer.[13]

Occurring in the context of an almost unbelievable tenderness,
a tenderness that is maternal rather than paternal, the rebuke
really hits. It reveals an affective force, a freedom of the heart
that can only spring from a clear awareness of man's fundamental identity as a creature wanted and loved by God the
Father. In Bernard the loss of this identity is qualified as *unlikeness*. Bernard never conceived of this unlikeness as a moral
problem. For him, the problem was always ontological. This is
what makes him great. In this he is a choice representative of
the Middle Ages as such, which characteristically entertained
a grandeur of vision and were more concerned with ontology
than with ethics. Ultimately, Bernard's great humanity is the
fruit of great humility. It marks him out. It reflects the love
of truth that feeds his vision of life and humanity. By keen
awareness of his limitations, he set his soul free and likewise
liberated his capacity for human love:

> As I ought, after the example of the Apostle, not to dominate
> over you, but only to rejoice with you, and as, according
> to the words of our Lord, we are all brothers having one
> Father in heaven, it is not improper for me to turn off from
> myself with the shield of truth the high names of lord and
> father with which you think to honor and not burden me,
> and appropriately call myself brother and fellow-servant as
> we share the same Father and the same condition.[14]

Bernard's notions of time and space are no less interesting.
He espouses the classical vision of time as a day "inspired"
(at creation) that "conspires" (through sin), "respires" (by
conversion), "expires" (in death), and "aspires" (with desire).
Hence temporal "space" seems to be limited to the "day" in
which memory, conscience, and desire unite in a perennially
lively dynamic of temporality opening onto eternity. However,
it is useful at the same time to recall his ideas on youth and
old age, tied up with the Gospel imagery of the earthly man
and the heavenly man:

> Inasmuch as we sin in three ways, by thought, speech, and
> works, our heart, mouth, and body are old. In our heart are
> carnal and worldly desires, that is, love of the flesh and love
> of the world. In our mouth, likewise, the old is present in
> two ways, by arrogance and calumny. Twofold it is in our
> body, too, through shamelessness and villainy. All these
> things are the image of the old man. All these things must
> be renewed in us. [. . .] Let our heart, then, be renewed
> from carnal and worldly desires so that, once these have
> been expunged, love of God and of the heavenly homeland
> may enter. Let arrogance and calumny withdraw from our
> mouth and their place be taken by confession of our sins
> and good esteem for our neighbor. Shamelessness and vil-
> lainy make our bodies old. Let continence and innocence
> replace them, so that each vice may be chased out by its
> contrary virtue. This renewal of which we have spoken is
> wrought by Christ's indwelling in us through faith, even
> as he himself says: "I make all things new!"[15]

In Bernard, *desire* stands for a space that separates time from eternity. The heart's intense desire covers the distance and, by hoping and waiting, fills the gap:

> With all my strength, I would follow the humble Jesus. I desire to hold in an embrace of vicarious love him who "loved me and gave himself up for me." Yet I must also eat the Paschal lamb. For unless I eat his flesh and drink his blood, I shall have no life in me. It is one thing to follow Jesus; it is another to hold him; yet another to eat him. To follow is a wholesome counsel. To hold and embrace is solemn joy. To eat is blessed life.[16]

This space, then, is also *home*. It is a domicile. Within it, Bernard distinguishes the tent, the courtyard, and the house. The *tent* has a roof but no foundation. It is portable, for there is no space for the just among the passing things of temporal existence, their inspired space is solely the Lord. The people's faith, which is their foundation, is not based on the things of this earth but on the Lord. The roof, meanwhile, signifies the covering and defence of divine grace. The vast *courtyard* that aligns the house is the space of those who have already abandoned the narrowness of the flesh. They breathe freely in the broad, open space of life. Bernard has in mind people who have already crossed the threshold of eternal life, but we may likewise think of those who, in the liberty of the Spirit, have entered the vast space of love. The courtyard, says Bernard, has a foundation but no roof. Why? Because the space of the courtyard is filled with God's love. It rests on the incorruptible base of faith, where man freely moves in love toward an infinite fulfilment. Finally, the *house* has neither roof nor foundation. Its foundation is eternal bliss; its roof is consummation and perfection. This house, home par excellence, is eternal life. But everything here below can become home as long as man is propelled by desire, acting through faith in the open, magnanimous space of love, toward the heavenly homeland.

❧ ❧ ❧

It is not easy, at this point, to single out the specific contribution of Cistercian thought and spirituality to the existential questioning of modern man. What can be unreservedly
established is that this monastic tradition is utterly humane.
It is keenly conscious of man's ontological status, grandeur,
and liberty. It is as truthful when it rejoices in humility as
when, in its momentum of irrepressible desire, so full of love
for God and humankind, it arrives at a gentle tenderness that
is simultaneously maternal and paternal. It cannot but offer
hope to the anguished hearts of our times. Of itself it gives
direction to our most intrinsic human yearning: the yearning
to correspond to our destiny.

Our History

We can get the measure of a given period of history by considering the way in which it regards the period that preceded it. A generation that paints the preceding generation all in black, blind to its moments of greatness and its necessary significance, cannot be anything but small-minded and wanting in self-confidence. [. . .] Any downgrading of the past implies an attempt to justify the void of the present.[1]

Living history is no less important than texts in giving us access to the Cistercian tradition with its rich and full humanity. History is our great teacher. Stanisław Grygiel once made the following observation in a talk to our community:

> Without the past the future is everything—and therefore nothing. Every revolution has endeavored to realize the future without a grounding in the past, without leaning on the past. Revolutions seek to obliterate the past. To put it differently, the life of a community, of a married couple, or of a family depends on a certain tradition. "Tradition," of course, does not refer to the past only, but also to the future. It is an all-embracing term. We cannot make and create the future by disregarding and forgetting the past. In order to know where I am going, I need to know where I am coming from, what my origins are.[2]

When I speak about history, I do not primarily speak of events. I speak of persons. I speak of the people who have constructed the historical space within which we live and move, and not only those sisters who have been entrusted by God with a prominent role, the abbesses and mistresses of novices. I speak

of all those members of our community and foundations who
have contributed to building up our churches. What would
have become of us, had we not known our seniors? I think of
Mother Giovanna, who labored faithfully in writing letters
to every single sister who went off on foundation, leaving by
way of signature a large red heart, the seal of a generative force
she had assumed with many tears but also with firm conviction. I think of Mother Margherita and her gift for creating a
warm, humane atmosphere through deeply personal relationships. I think of the spirit of sacrifice that marked the lives of
a Mother Agostina, a Mother Annunziata through relentless
work in the kitchen and orchard. We are all indebted to the
humanity and holiness of the sisters who have gone before us.
How can a community possibly turn its mind to the heavenly
Jerusalem without envisaging the sisters who served their
earthly Jerusalem in the humble joy of self-giving, building
up the city through daily fidelity? In this chapter, therefore,
my aims are these:

- to render present and relevant the pedagogical patrimony
  left us by those who have gone before me in the abbatial
  ministry I am currently trying to exercise;

- to confront this patrimony with our present experience of
  the manifold reality of our Cistercian foundations, often
  situated far away;

- to enrich our patrimony by reflecting on the experience
  that has led us to maturity in the school of our own
  history.

To this end I shall refer to a small number of creative, faithful
individuals who, through love and self-giving, managed to
convey intelligent understanding of our Cistercian history,
charism, and grace. On the basis of an extant patrimony, they
created a particular mode of transmission, a pedagogy all
their own, in order to invest an already life-giving truth with
impulses of newness and current relevance.

Mother Pia and What Set Her Apart

We need look only slightly beyond our immediate past to
come upon the commanding figure of Mother Pia Gullini, abbess of Grottaferrata from 1931 to 1940 and again from 1946
to 1951. Regarding the monastic pedagogy proper to Vitorchiano, Mother Pia is especially interesting, for she represents
a milestone on the path of the community that has given us
life. When we consider the paltry reality of our origins (in the
community of San Vito, founded in 1875 and later transferred
to Grottaferrata), we find several moving signs of the path's
early development. Mother Pia fostered these signs. She consolidated the reality they represented by virtue of prophetic
strength and an immense capacity for maternity. What kind
of signs am I talking about? I have in mind the minute Sister
Gerarda (1877–1904), who would take on a whole herd of
giddy cows, calming them down with the innocent force of
total obedience; Sister Giuseppina (1876–1904), who converted
her naturally rebellious spirit by humbly accepting "any"
indication given by her superiors, even when harsh or seem-
ingly unreasonable; Sister Geltrude (1876–1904), who would
run to the abbess to share any extraneous thought that was
churning in her heart, so as to dash the enemy's stratagems
against the rock of Christ; or Sister Zaccaria, who tempered
the fatigue of the orchard with the enchanting certainty that
the Blessed Virgin would await her at the gate of paradise with
a cup of incomparable sweet wine to season the dry bread of
her labor. These humble, unknown lives left deep furrows in
which future seeds could grow. Copious water, sweat, and
blood flowed into these furrows, forming a living brook that
poured right into the great heart of Mother Pia.

Several disparate elements combined to forge her personality: the culture and sensibility of the *haute bourgeoisie* into
which she was born; a broad social and human experience
that allowed her to cultivate her keen interest in sport, quite in
the face of the restrictive ideas of her time; a rare sense of the
Church that made of her a catechist fit to proclaim Jesus Christ

even in the most disreputable and dangerous neighborhoods of the Roman suburbs. This synthesis was finally formed by a slowly emerging monastic vocation. Once Mother Pia had embraced it, at the cost of great labor, she lived it out lovingly, with uncompromising fidelity to the rigid observance that marked her French monastic formation at Laval. Her encounter with Trappist monasticism was an encounter of grace. She identified profoundly with the austere poverty of the monastery, with the strict silence interrupted only by liturgical chant, with the hard manual labor and the strong common life that embraced every aspect of existence. Her soul was forged by such practices. She loved Laval, the monastery in which she was trained, though her love was seasoned with pain. Inadequate means of transport and communication meant that she never saw her family, whom she held in great affection. She suffered from this and from being away from her homeland. At the same time, the religious art of the period, which filled churches and cloisters, even monastic cells, with suffocating, bigoted statuary and nauseating paintings, inflicted a real wound on her artist's soul. Above all, she had to contend with her own personality, which was by nature rebellious, original, vivacious, and independent. She strove to contain it within the narrow path of obedience, regulated in every detail by the *Usages* that were still in force.

All this was to prove precious and useful in preparing her to face her own destiny. It entailed the transfer from Laval, the prestigious flagship of the Order, with a high level of culture and a discerning monastic observance, to the poor reality of Grottaferrata. Certainly, a great spirit of faith and an uncommon capacity for sacrifice marked Grottaferrata, but it was culturally impoverished, muddled in its observance, and struggling to make a living. It cannot have been easy. From this mixture of grace and contradictions, grief and high ideals, Mother Pia extracted the wisdom she transmitted to the community while serving first as novice mistress, then as superior. Her teaching flowed from lived experience and was enriched by intuition. With passion and conviction she succeeded in passing on what to this day defines the orientation of our community, even though we have not always entirely understood or accepted her teaching.

Mother Pia's love of humility and her option for humiliation were quite out of the ordinary. Sister Fara, our community's humble, intelligent chronicler, tells of a revealing incident that occurred when Mother Pia was thirteen years old. Having been carried off by a flight of vanity, she declared with customary resolve that, "in order to learn humility, I would be quite prepared to go off and bury myself in a convent." Once in the monastery, humility became the foundation of her experience and hence of her monastic teaching. When the superiors of our Order, skeptical of Mother Pia's increasingly public role in the Italian and European Church, ordered her to leave Grottaferrata for the Swiss abbey of La Fille-Dieu, she smiled at the great old chestnut tree that had just been cut down from its place in the cloister because it stole the light, and mused: "You see how easy it is to disappear from view! It is simply a matter of striking at the roots." The anthropological teaching of Cîteaux does presuppose an accurate understanding of humility and obedience. It considers man to be created in the image of God, insists that this image is indelibly stamped on his being, and recognizes its expression in the freedom and dignity of the sons of God. Mother Pia appropriated this Cistercian wisdom as if by instinct. She made it the radical criterion by which she measured herself, her behavior, and her discernment.

A second distinguishing feature of Mother Pia was her great gift for maternity. The sisters who lived with her remember myriad small gestures of motherly solicitude. Mother Giovanna recounts how "when we returned from the vineyard exhausted and drenched in sweat she was there at the gate, waiting for us with some simple refreshment (we had nothing!) that expressed her great love, a small piece of candy or chocolate or half a bread roll with jam." From Sister Francesca

we know that "she always asked me, who was the youngest
of the laysisters, to share my impressions of the novices who
worked with me in the poultry pen. She really wanted me to
say what I thought." The respectful attention of her maternal
heart is revealed not least in the last manuscript notes she
drew up at La Fille-Dieu in answer to various questions put to
her about Blessed Maria Gabriella, whose heroic self-offering
for Christian unity was attracting great interest. Reading these
simple notes, one is struck by the tenderness with which she
refers to Gabriella as *la mia figliola*, "my little girl." We only
have to read Mother Pia's description of Gabriella's physical
appearance to be touched by her motherly perspective:

> Her mouth was rather large, but her smile was gentle and
> surprisingly lovely, revealing a set of regular, white, and
> healthy teeth. Her broad chin indicated natural wilfulness.
> Seen at an angle, she had a classical profile that sometimes
> attracted the admiring gaze of the artist in me. It was as if I
> caught sight once again of the models I had drawn during
> my years of study, when I was a young woman.

There is also the endearing admiration with which she speaks
of Gabriella's gift for gratitude, which Mother Pia considered
an expression of her *figliola*'s radical fidelity:

> Thank you! Thank you! The gratitude that had always
> characterized Gabriella was extended to become a sea into
> which her soul dove, disappearing beneath the surface,
> never again to emerge. The words she used to express her
> thankfulness were invariably simple and modest, yet car-
> ried the resonance of the depth from which they sprang.

Mother Pia is clearly moved by the phrase Gabriella once
used in response to a sister who was famous for her stubborn-
ness: "As far as I am concerned, once the superior has said
something, I cannot bring myself to think differently." These
are simple notes intended to complement the biography of
Mother Giovanna Dore. They were never meant to constitute

a narrative in their own right. For our present purposes, it is not even the reference to Blessed Gabriella that especially interests us but rather the attention paid by Mother Pia to a sister's physical and spiritual characteristics. Only a mother's heart can perceive these details so acutely, so movingly. Her motherliness was totally oriented toward the growth of her daughters in authentic obedience and liberating gratitude. It could rejoice in the tiniest gesture of docility and cordial thankfulness. At the same time she did not hesitate to administer severe admonition and correction. All the sisters recall instances of Mother Pia's "sacred rage," outbursts that were not always understood by the person they struck, considered by the abbess to be holding back from entering a new space of interior freedom through attachment to some minute possession (such as a piece of soap, the most precious commodity of the period) or to her own judgment. Still, Mother Pia's "sacred rage" revealed a passionate maternity that engendered a whole generation of saints. Blessed Gabriella is but the choice flower mysteriously appointed by God to witness to the silent sanctity that flourished in the humble day-to-day life at Grottaferrata, where a number of beloved sisters, swept away by tuberculosis or wartime deprivation, quickly reached heaven in a state of genuine holiness.

Mother Pia's third defining feature was a vast and profound sense of the Church. Underpinned by firm intuition, it decisively shaped her teaching and her very way of interacting with the community. The ecclesial vision that characterized the community, its enlightened *sensus ecclesiae*, is revealed in the spontaneous simplicity with which Mother Immacolata or Blessed Gabriella caught on to the ecumenical calling that stirred in the heart of Mother Pia and responded to it with conviction and lucidity, assuming as a matter of course the offering of their lives for their separated brethren. Mother Agostina, who died in 1999, often showed us the holy card Mother Pia gave her as a memento when, at the same time as Blessed Gabriella, she offered her life for the unity of the Church. God immediately

assumed Sister Gabriella's offering. Mother Agostina would
bring hers slowly to perfection until the age of almost ninety.
However, the two sisters' offering, the memory they both kept
with veneration, sprang from the same ecclesial, ecumenical
vision, which had penetrated the entire community and profoundly touched the hearts of entire generations of nuns at
Grottaferrata. It was no coincidence that Sister Leonarda, who
was thirty when she died, offered her life for the Holy Father
with moving lucidity. The pope was informed of her offering
and wrote back through the Secretariat of State: "My heart is
especially consoled by the fact that these religious, totally given
to a life of prayer and mortification, remember the pope before
the Lord with such filial charity, such devout self-sacrifice." And
how can we forget the prayer made intermittently by Sister
Maura in her agony when, close to death, she kept repeating:
"O Lord, convert every soul! Let no one be lost!"

From within the poverty and littleness of Grottaferrata rises
this tangible revelation of an immense love for the Church.
Here we are still, naturally, in preconciliar times and cannot
yet expect to recognize the consciousness of "being Church"
that will flourish among later generations at Vitorchiano. But
already the Church is present in fullness as mother, teacher,
inspiration, and guide, as the sacred body of the Lord. There
is no sentimental devotion attached to these various aspects
of the Church, which nonetheless motivate, shape, and determine the monastic vocation of a community. They combine to
form a living pedagogy. Considering its salient features, we
are immediately faced with three fundamental values: *humility*, *maternity*, and *a profound grounding in the Church*. These are
the notions that will accompany us throughout our history,
throughout our growth as a community.

Mother Pia's Heritage

Mother Pia has certainly left an imprint on our lives, though
we shall understand its full significance only with the pass-

ing of time. The abbesses who have followed her, too, have transmitted messages of their own, less easy to evaluate than that of Mother Pia, but nonetheless directing the living flow of the community. To speak specifically of *monastic* teaching, all the sisters know the passionate insistence on charity that characterized Mother Immacolata Tiraboschi, who was abbess from 1953 to 1958. The sisters, she would say, must constantly choose to love one another, they must attain to the freedom that gives the heart room to breathe. Such recurrent aspects of her governance remain with us as a living memory. "The Trappist life?" she would say: "Yes, of course, it entails dying, but with great gentleness." Charity and freedom are, clearly, values very dear to the entire living tradition of Cîteaux.

Mother Armanda Borroni was abbess of our community from 1959 to 1964. We remember her for her inexhaustible gratitude, expressed humbly and spontaneously to everyone. She seemed never to say anything but "Thank you." Her simplicity and apparent poverty made her pass almost unnoticed, but it was by her intelligent, silent effort that the community of Grottaferrata could put down roots at Vitorchiano, ploughing their fields and their own hearts to receive the numerous vocations of those years. With admirable continuity, Mother Armanda was able to graft the postwar generations onto the ancient trunk of Cîteaux. The old learned to understand the young; the young learned to understand the old.

Can we point to certain constant pedagogical values stressed during Mother Armanda's tenure? We recognize an emphasis on charity, freedom, and gratitude; we see a confidence in the young, a culture of serious work, and an effort, still feeling its way, to ensure good formation. The Rule of Saint Benedict remained a primary reference, while the Cistercian Fathers were brought into focus through the teaching of sisters whose gifts Mother Armanda was quick to esteem: none of us will ever forget the very first "patristic chapters" given by Mother Ignazia, her young prioress. We witness above all the transmission of a way of life marked by hospitality and openness, continuity, faithfulness, a broad horizon, and a great capacity for listening.

The development of a monastic pedagogy at an intellectual, conceptual level, the development of a method and a manner of thinking, began a few years later, in response to the development of the Order as a whole. This development was articulated in the documents of key General Chapters after the Council and in the new Constitutions. With us, it found expression in the life-giving enterprise of making new foundations that would come to characterize our community's vocation. The documents of the General Chapters from 1969 to 1971 called for a careful revision of the quality of monastic life in our Cistercian monasteries, asking us to be creative and responsible in interiorizing the Order's charism. At the same time, our foundations required us to formulate a clear idea of what we, as a founding house, wanted to pass on as authentic, constitutive elements of our monastery's charism and grace, as distinct from those elements that spring from local culture, from traditions and customs that are merely provisional and rooted in circumstances.

Very probably, all the houses of the Order followed a similar path in response to the new, ecclesial mentality of the Second Vatican Council, but for Vitorchiano the process was especially urgent and necessary. At the time we were receiving a large number of vocations. These had in large measure been nurtured by the New Movements and entertained a new sense of the Church. A break with the past marked the postwar generations. They contributed to broadening our outlook on life, ushering in a more complex sensibility and culture, a fresh perspective on the problems faced by the young. In this way the community was taught to attend to and discern both the general "signs of the times" and the unique, singular contribution of each individual.

Around 1970 Vitorchiano was certainly a poor community. At the same time, it was a community open to embrace the newness of history and the new generations who came bringing along their questions, challenges, and peculiar grace. We were able to integrate these elements into the living reality of our monastic journey, for at the heart of our community we carried what today we would call a "culture of life"; that is, we had a corporate identity ready to receive respectfully and without prejudice any contribution that could truly help the community to mature. Certain elements, as old as monastic life itself yet freshly perceived, were delineated very soon:

- *Obedience*, no longer understood principally as fidelity to usages and customs set to regulate life in infinitesimal detail, but as *adherence* to the particular grace of the community, as *faithfulness* to the authority of the house, and as *mutual gift* in the context of a common life that binds all members together in a shared process of conversion.

- From this flowed a new understanding of *relationships in community*, stressing trust, the pursuit of communion, positive attitudes, sincere friendship, mutual esteem, and a readiness to serve.

- Finally, the very notion of authority began to appear in a different light, as a point of reference and a criterion by which to evaluate our behavior and our vocation, with the abbess emerging as the community's *spiritual mother*.

By virtue of the very force of renewal they carried, these elements were inevitably misunderstood and criticized. Something new was stirring and coming to life at the heart of our community without clamorous contradictions, without rupture and refusal, yet with an irreversible momentum. Fears were expressed that our emphasis on communion and integration into community was inimical to the autonomy and liberty of persons, who need space in order to express themselves and be creative, as if a process of genuine integration presupposes the coercion of individual freedom. When we started practicing dialogue and a shared revision of life, this was considered an attack on the values of silence and solitude so typical of Trappist living. There were even some who thought our exchanges compromised the freedom of conscience, given the climate of freedom of expression and the profound search for individual and corporate truth: "These young things use community dialogues to share what belongs under the seal of confession!"

Today we smile at the thought of such taboos, which made for a valuable crucible of pain and purification. Thanks to this crucible we clearly and humbly witnessed the birth of a shared experience of formation, a shared vision that was fit to endure. Only life can generate life. We embrace life insofar as we accept the small deaths of each day as an oblation freely given, as a bridge to eternity.

The development of Vitorchiano's particular pedagogy owes much to the insight and generous service of several novice mistresses who have followed one another during these past thirty years. The first to find herself receiving the new, postwar generations was Mother Franca. She began a small but stubborn battle against the idea that the sole measure of a sister's spirit of sacrifice was her staying power for hard labor in the fields. The famous motto, "Offer yourself up for God," was common currency. It was translated into concrete reality as "Offer yourself up to work" and was regarded as a sure path to sanctity. Mother Franca was faced with a different kind of youth, with real potential for spiritual growth but less physical endurance for manual labor in the fields. What characterized her was not so much a new line of teaching as a courageous, generous charism of maternity that sought to provide room for a diversity that, far from betraying the monastic charism, sought new openings behind the austere face of Trappist life. Following the spirit of the time, she strove to lighten the fasts and to make the observance of nocturnal Vigils less hard. As an alternative to heavy farm work, she found other expressions of service in which the young could exercise their generosity.

Little by little we were able to structure the famous "intervals" of the novices into ordered periods of *lectio divina* and study. We even (and this was a true revolution!) made use of the sacrosanct time set aside for manual work to provide courses of formation and thus succeeded in formulating a real *ratio studiorum*. Through all this, the relationship between the novice mistress and the young in formation grew deeper. Vocational discernment at the various stages shifted from authoritative observation to a qualitative assessment of individual persons and the motivation that sustained their commitment. The year 1970 saw the inauguration of the *monasticate*, a time during which the simply professed are accompanied toward full integration into the community. The aim of the monasticate is to offer the sisters individual formation while helping them to grow into the mutual acceptance that will underpin any future integration into the community. We aimed to communicate an ever-more interiorized, responsible understanding of the Cistercian charism and of the specific grace of our community. At the time, we formulated a list of questions for discernment. These served us well for quite a period:

- Overall aim for the *first year*: growth in *self-knowledge*. How do you see yourself in the light of your God-given vocation and the demands entailed by that vocation?

- Overall aim for the *second year*: growth in *knowledge of the community*. How do you see the community you are about to enter fully? Can you wholly accept it the way it really is? How does the community assist or impede your own conversion? What does it mean for you to "belong" to this particular community?

- Overall aim for the *third year*: growth in *knowledge of the vows* fostered by an awareness of personal responsibility. What do the vows mean to you? What does it mean to pronounce them definitively and forever? Do you consider that they truly define who you are before God, before others, and with regard to yourself?

After making our first two foundations (at Valserena, near Pisa in Italy, and at Hinojo in Argentina), the monasticate embarked on a thorough formation in *humility*, understood as the truth about oneself, about the vocation received, and about one's behavior in everyday life. It inculcated a responsible *interiorization* of the monastic vocation and the values that define it, seeing it not as "normative" but rather as "constitutive" of the person called by God. Finally, the monasticate sought to foster genuine *fidelity* to the house and the authority of the house, a fidelity without hesitations or ambiguities, guided by the recognition that a monk's fundamental identity is defined by obedience.

What we especially remember from this period is the passion for what we now would refer to as our "common vision." In those days we referred to it as "obedience of judgment" or as a search for "community consensus." As a community we came to regard a simply executive authority with some skepticism, for such authority can do little to foster true obedience if it does not lead our judgment to mature so as to be transformed into a genuine commitment of the heart. A battle was joined against every kind of sublimation that concealed our fears or our shame when we were faced with our own inner conflicts, thus blocking the free and strong expression of truth.

It was at this time that we began to realize the cohesive potential of the generational groups that made up successive monasticates, forming a dynamic that would later come to define our monastic pedagogy. We adopted the following insight as a guiding principle: "If a sister cannot be really integrated among the members of her own generational group, she will never become a fully integrated member of the community as a whole." At the same time there flourished a capacity for positive insight that encouraged each person to give her best. Any tendency to withdraw to the margins of the community was sternly censored, as were expressions of self-justification that, while masquerading under the name of charity or high spirituality, in fact represented a conflict with authority. An intelligent, attentive openness to the Order was a further feature of those years. The official documents of the Order, like those of the Second Vatican Council, became the basis on which Vitorchiano's formative enterprise grew.

Already in the years from 1975 to 1980 a remarkably coherent pedagogy was evidenced. The generations that benefited from it were later able to convey its message effectively, while constantly enriching it with new insights gained from openness to the signs of the times. It goes without saying that there were contradictions, toil, and mistakes along the way. Not everything, perhaps, was clear, consistent, and self-evident. Never have we more strongly perceived *tradition* as a foundational value. At the same time, the newness of language and procedures gave rise to understandable anxiety. The principal grace has been the grace of continuity. Thanks to it, the community humbly accepted the challenge posed by the times and by its own corporate judgment. With patient obedience it worked out a monastic pedagogy whose validity has been amply confirmed by the experience of subsequent years.

In order to better understand this labor of teaching and transmission, we shall now cast a quick glance at the path followed by our Order in the twentieth century. It will help us to situate certain key insights within the parameters of a historical process that exceeds by far the modest reality of our community.

Learning from History 1
Cistercian Monasticism in the First Half of the Twentieth Century

Can we learn from our history? Yes, we can, for the history of our Order has been made by men and women who, grounded in the faith of Abraham, have sought eternal answers to the most important questions posed by their earthly pilgrimage. We do not intend, here, to write the history of Cîteaux. Our intention is simply to reflect briefly on a few individuals who have played leading roles in Cistercian monastic history in the twentieth century.

Once, while at Vitorchiano we were studying the *Exordium Magnum*, a foundational Cistercian text of the early thirteenth century, we made the observation that,

> Cîteaux is a gift of Christ to the Church. In the eleventh century, it was the place in which the deepest hopes for renewal and reform of an entire era were made incarnate: "In these last days, the all-powerful and merciful Lord has planted the seed of his grace in the wilderness of Cîteaux. Watered by the rain of the Spirit, this seed has expanded much and acquired spiritual substance, growing into a tree so large, lovely, and fruitful that the peoples, tribes, and tongues of many nations find rest in its shadow and rejoice to eat their fill of its fruit."[1]

The Order's history in any given period is grafted onto this gift. It is the same charism that flourishes throughout the centuries, offering repose to human hearts anxiously searching for happiness.

Regarding the Order's history in the first fifty years of the twentieth century, we have nothing to add to the magisterial expositions provided by Thomas Merton in *The Waters of Siloe* and by Louis Lekai in *The Cistercians*. Naturally, the Order felt the devastating impact of the two World Wars of 1914 to 1918 and 1939 to 1945. The Spanish Civil War from 1936 to 1939 likewise affected it deeply. In the face of these tragedies, our Cistercian monasteries saw a genuine flowering of martyrs and saints. It was a silent flowering, obscured by the bloody turmoil of global conflict; yet there can be no doubt that, through it, the mysterious designs of Providence prepared the lively heritage we benefit from today. The Order's immediate past is no less charged with the energy of purification and holiness than was the period of the French Revolution or that of the migrations headed by Augustin de Lestrange. We need only think of the many monks who were massacred in the Spanish Civil War, whose cause of beatification is well underway; of the many who lost their lives in the two World Wars; of those who perished in Nazi concentration camps, like Father Nivard of Koeningshoven-Tilburg and his five brothers and sisters; of the collective martyrdom of our monastery of Our Lady of Consolation in China between 1947 and 1953. These numerous examples show the sap that was rising in our Order's roots in the first half of the twentieth century. In the midst of such troubled waves of violence we see a handful of exceptional individuals emerging as bright guiding stars. It is to these monks and nuns we shall now briefly refer, for it is evident that the Order has drawn life from their teaching and example.

The beginning of the twentieth century witnessed a movement away from the rigid reformed observance of La Valsainte to a rediscovery of our Cistercian roots. It was a movement initiated by Dom Jean-Baptiste Chautard, abbot of Sept-Fons; by Dom Vital Lehodey, abbot of Bricquebec; and by Dom Anselme Le Bail, abbot of Scourmont. Their efforts prepared the ground for the evolutionary process in which the Order is

currently involved. The towering, prophetic figure of Thomas
Merton seals, as it were, this half-century, marking the end of
an era and looking ahead to something new and yet unknown.
Beside these great men I would like to place Mother Pia Gullini, who, as superior of Sister Maria Gabriella, directed the
destiny of a saint, while her own life bore the imprint of a
singular mystery of suffering and visionary insight.

Dom Jean-Baptiste Chautard (1858–1935)

Dom Chautard entered the abbey of Aiguebelle in 1877 and it
did not take long until he was appointed superior of Cham-
barand, which at the time was struggling financially. He was
elected abbot of Sept-Fons in 1897, still a young man of thirty-
nine, with rare gifts of government and financial administration. He was to head the community of Sept-Fons for thirty-six
years. Dom Chautard was a man of his time. In engaging with
the civil authority and with the concrete reality of turn-of-the-
century French society, he showed an openness that was free,
well-informed, and truthful. He defended the autonomy of
individual monasteries, while lucidly envisaging the future
of the Order and the making of new foundations. He himself
made a start at setting up a house in Brazil.

Dom Chautard was a profoundly contemplative man. Faced
as he was with the lingering shadow of Jansenism and with
new forms of atheism, he felt the need to spread far and wide
a simple spiritual teaching that could be easily understood.
With that in mind he wrote *The Soul of the Apostolate*. He was
unafraid to embrace new discoveries. In 1932 he opened the
doors of Sept-Fons to the shooting of an early sound film.
As someone who not only possessed profound knowledge
of Christian doctrine and spirituality but also had learned to
master his own personality, he became a real spiritual father.

The extreme austerity of monastic life at the time gave him
little scope to express his sensitive nature. He never failed,
however, even when on a journey, to remember the feast days

of the brethren and wrote faithfully to those of his monks who were engaged in military service. He had a special love for the least, most unimposing brethren. With a sure spiritual instinct, he knew how to pass beyond appearances in order to recognize men of quality. He did not hesitate to entrust responsibility to a man who could carry it, should he be the last of the laybrothers. With healthy realism he did what he could to ensure financial independence both for his own community and for other monasteries, considering this to be a necessary condition for a life given to God.

In Dom Chautard, then, we find salient signs of a new tendency in monastic leadership. We see a way of thinking that valued the life of contemplation higher than physical austerity. We see an intelligent engagement with secular society and the search for means of subsistence adequate to ensure contemplative freedom. Above all, we see an abbot who understands and exercises his authority as genuine spiritual fatherhood.[2]

Dom Vital Lehodey (1857–1948)

Dom Lehodey was of the same generation as Dom Chautard. He was born at Hambye in 1857, into a very poor family. Aged twenty-three he was ordained a diocesan priest. Ten years later, in July 1890, he entered the monastery of Bricquebec. He was elected abbot in 1895 and remained in office until 1929. It is interesting to see how a man so strongly attracted to an ideal of austerity (to the extent that he irreversibly ruined his own health) gradually and through prayer discovered humility of heart as the surest path to love. Dom Lehodey referred to two authorities. The first was the Rule of Saint Benedict, which he scrutinized with passion in order to discover the secret depth of its spiritual teaching. The second was his tender devotion to the Child Jesus. Having at first tended to regard God more as a stern Judge than as a Father, his devotion to the Child Jesus gave him a different perspective on the spiritual life:

He revealed to me the goodness of his heart, his love and
tenderness, his mercy and meekness, his amazing simplicity, so many things that render him lovable and attractive
in his sacred humanity. And in this very way he revealed
to me his divinity. His humanity is, indeed, a most faithful
mirror in which the infinite perfections of his divinity are
painted in smaller format. All that we see, as in a miniature,
in his childhood, is infinitely present in the Word. And since
the Word is the splendor of the Father and the image of his
goodness, I came, by knowing the little Jesus, likewise to
know the Father and the Holy Spirit, for all three are but
one and the same infinite charity. The sweet childhood of
my little Jesus has thus been for me like the Beautiful Gate
by which he let me enter a little—alas! only a little—into
the inner sanctuary of the Godhead.[3]

Several books flowed from this spirituality, such as the *Spiritual
Directory*, the *Ways of Mental Prayer*, and *Holy Abandonment*.

The art and chief labor of spirituality, our applying it (as we
purpose) to every moment of our life, should thus consist
in descent. We must descend, and descend ever further
right to the heart of blessed littleness. We must work cease-
lessly through obedience and humility *to become little, to let
ourselves be made little*, as much as God will permit, in any
way he pleases, by whatever hand he chooses to employ.
[. . .] In this way he will lead us fast and far along the path
of perfection.

This, from then on, was the grace Dom Lehodey sought to
obtain "by means of blessed littleness, with filial obedience
and holy abandonment."[4] There can be no doubt that insights
such as these altered the spiritual climate of the Order, preparing the way for profound developments.

Dom Anselme Le Bail (1878–1956)

Having entered the Belgian abbey of Scourmont in 1904, Anselme Le Bail was elected its abbot in 1913. He fought in the

First World War, then returned to his abbey in 1919. In 1928
he made Scourmont's first foundation on the Welsh island of
Caldey. Seven years later he hoped to make a further foundation in India, but the Second World War ruled out any such
idea. During the war years, the community of Scourmont was
exiled twice, with Dom Le Bail firmly at the helm. He spent
his last seven years, from 1949 to 1956, suffering the results of
a stroke, which left him deprived of speech. He endured this
trial with a patience and gentleness that were the supreme
proof of his monastic genius.

Dom Le Bail's teaching, ever both clear and profound, was
based on the liturgy, the Rule of Saint Benedict, and the Cistercian Fathers, in whose regard he cultivated a robustly historical approach. Thomas Merton called him

> a man of deep spirituality and learning who had penetrated
> far into the theology of the Cistercian writers of the twelfth
> century. Taking them as his commentators on the Rule of
> Saint Benedict, he had evolved a clear and well-ordered
> spiritual doctrine, by the light of which he was able to give
> his novices a more thoroughly Cistercian intellectual for-
> mation than they could find anywhere in the Order except,
> perhaps, at Sept-Fons, where Dom Chautard was abbot.
> The novitiate at Chimay was filled with a spirit of balance
> and sanity; a spirit of simplicity, of clarity; it was eminently
> Benedictine, and one thing dominated all: the love and ser-
> vice of Christ.[5]

A wave of humanity, an entirely new sensibility, was washing
over the Order. Merton indicates the impact of this formation
by introducing a brief case study of Maxime Carlier, a young
monk trained by Anselme Le Bail, who would soon be forced
to leave the monastery by the roll call of a cruel war:

> No doubt all these things had been present ever since
> De Rancé's reform, but they were buried, cramped in
> other elements which might have proved dangerous and
> had, indeed, had bad effects on temperaments like that of
> Frater Maxime. There were many like him in France. He

was intelligent, generous, yet there was something in his nature that tended to warp the spiritual life out of its true direction—a certain rigorism, a harshness that chilled the heart and bred suspicion of God, instead of love. Perhaps there was some germ of Jansenism there that tended to breed suspicion between his soul and God—but it was only a germ, and in the healthy atmosphere of Chimay the germ did not prosper. [. . .] The influence of his father master was supplemented by the reading of Saint Gertrude, from whom Frater Maxime learned a doctrine that can be summed up in two words: confidence and love. [. . .] One day he realized suddenly that he was a new man. He had learned the real meaning of God's love, and he saw that, until then, he had been crawling on the ground, while now he seemed to fly.[6]

The example of Maxime Carlier reveals not only the particular climate of Scourmont, but the transformation that, between the World Wars, took place throughout the Order. Dom Anselme Le Bail stood at the heart of this maturing process, which in part sprang from changes in society, but no less from a profound assimilation of the spirit of Cîteaux:

The influence of this remarkable person at General Chapters of the Order was in no way negligible. It would have been greater still had [Dom Le Bail] not met with the clear, lasting opposition of some who held firmly to the Usages and Customary while making insufficient reference to the tradition of spirituality. These men disapproved of Le Bail's notions, which they dismissed as intellectualism prone to laxity, too adventurous in their insistence on freedom and the reasonable 'autonomy' that the abbot of Scourmont not only bore with but actively sought to cultivate. His nonconformist liberty could cause astonishment. No one, however, doubted his uprightness, humility, and obedience. He was universally revered for his readiness to be of service and for his thoughtful charity, even with regard to those who had but slight sympathy for his ideas. Later, in the wake of the Second Vatican Council, his prophetic views gained greater acceptance and their impact was felt far and wide.[7]

With these brief indications I have intended to show that later developments in the Order, under the generalate of Dom Gabriel Sortais and after the Second Vatican Council, build on a tradition with deep roots. A whole line of prophets and saints prepared the way for what was to come. At the summit of this trajectory we find the commanding presence of Thomas Merton. We have all, to some extent, been raised in his school. Our present understanding of the Cistercian vocation owes much to him, even though it is easy to recognize that his vision was sometimes naïve and marked by contradiction.

Thomas Merton (1915–1968)

In an article from 1986, Charles Dumont cites amply from two of Merton's books, *The Sign of Jonas* and *Thoughts in Solitude*.[8] Two passages from these books reveal Thomas Merton's monastic heart with singular clarity:

> I have always overshadowed Jonas with my mercy, and cruelty I have known not at all. Have you had sight of Me, Jonas, My child? Mercy within mercy within mercy. I have forgiven the universe without end, because I have never known sin. [. . .] Do not lay up for yourself ecstasies upon earth, where time and space corrupt, where the minutes break in and steal. No more lay hold on time, Jonas, My son, lest the rivers bear you away. What was fragile has become powerful. I loved what was most frail. I looked upon what was nothing. I touched what was without substance, and within what was not, I am.[9]

And again:

> There is no true spiritual life outside the love of Christ. [. . .] If we know how great is the love of Jesus for us we will never be afraid to go to Him in all our poverty. [. . .] The surest sign that we have received a spiritual understanding of God's love for us is the appreciation of our own poverty in the light of his infinite mercy. We must love our own poverty as Jesus loves it.[10]

Merton's idea of the contemplative life started forming from
the outset of his monastic life. Writes Brother Patrick Hart:
"He saw it as the full flowering of the Christian life." And he
goes on to cite an unpublished manuscript titled *The Interior
Experience*:

> The first thing to do, before even thinking of contemplation,
> is to try to recover your natural unity in its basic elements,
> to integrate your compartmentalized being into a whole
> that is coordinated and simple, to learn to live like a uni-
> fied human person. First of all, this means gathering up the
> fragments of your scattered, distracted existence so that,
> when you say "I," there is really something there to prop
> up the pronoun you use.[11]

On this foundation of realism Thomas Merton set off to become what Léon Bloy would call a "pilgrim of the absolute."
He was a man who constantly posed searching questions
about his vocation while trying hard to find good answers. At
the same time he realized that the radical, definitive answer
was in fact provided by the very vocation he was questioning:
"All things change, and die and disappear. Questions arrive,
assume their actuality, and die and also disappear. In this hour
I shall cease to ask them, and silence shall be my answer."[12]

If we may speak of Thomas Merton's influence on the development of the Order (in my opinion, it has been immense),
it consists above all in his constant effort to bring out the essential components of the monastic vocation. Merton basically
called on us to live out an unconditional gift of ourselves to
God that goes beyond the formal observance of obedience.
By belonging utterly to God, we belong, too, to the rest of
mankind, as he pointed out in his final conference in Bangkok:

> This kind of monasticism cannot be extinguished. It is im-
> perishable. It represents an instinct of the human heart, and
> it represents a charism given by God to man. It cannot be
> rooted out, because it does not depend on man. It does not
> depend on cultural factors, and it does not depend on socio-

logical or psychological factors. It is something much deeper. I, as a monk—and, I think, you as monks—can agree that we believe this to be the deepest and most essential thing in our lives, and because we believe this, we have given ourselves to the kind of life we have adopted. I believe that our renewal consists precisely in deepening this understanding and this grasp of that which is most real.[13]

Mother Pia Gullini (1892–1959)

I should like to add a few final words about Mother Pia Gullini, whose teaching and personality we touched on in the previous chapter. She was a Cistercian of strong mettle. She was ascetical and austere, a lover of the Eucharist, an intuitive and careful teacher, at once tenderly maternal and abruptly demanding. She formed Blessed Maria Gabriella and a small army of other young nuns, many of whom were swept away by war and raging tuberculosis. These nuns died holy deaths, though they will never officially be proclaimed saints. Mother Pia's passionate teaching left its mark on them all. The abbess would require a fidelity to the Rule and *Usages* that was based on intelligent conviction. At the same time, she would indicate a spiritual perspective vast enough to embrace the Church and the whole world. Thereby she led her nuns to appreciate the missionary dimension of their cloistered calling. Mother Pia's temperament, like that of all men and women touched by genius, was intense and not always coherent. What interests us most in this woman of culture and broad views is her sense of the Church, what we might call her ecclesial instinct. For Mother Pia's own community and for the foundations made by Vitorchiano, this heritage remains especially tangible and dear. Mother Pia's instant understanding of the initiatives of Paul Watson and Paul Couturier, two men promoting an initiative of prayer for the return of all Christians to Catholic unity, was but one dimension of her life of oblation to the Church and for the Church. All who came to her for advice received the same answer: "Love the humanity of Christ; give all for the good of the Church." Many recall the realism of a phrase she often repeated: "Our worth consists in what we are before God, no more, no less, whether others hold us in esteem or disdain. Once this principle is clear in our minds, our lives acquire great energy, great freedom of spirit." Shortly before her death, she cited, in a few handwritten notes, a phrase of Monsignor Gay's:

> Insofar as we live out a love for all, destroying to the best of our ability everything within us and around us that hinders unity, we accomplish in our own small way the prayer of Christ "that they may all be one" (John 17:21). We participate in the mystery by which the Father lovingly receives the Son's prayer, bestowing upon it an efficacious power.

Conclusion

Why have we chosen to remember these particular individuals in our rapid overview of Cistercian monasticism in the first half of the twentieth century? Because they, alongside many others whom space does not permit us to mention, cleared a new path of transformation and holiness. In remembering them, we notice a continuous development away from the mortifying austerity that dominated the beginning of the century, an austerity intent on disciplining the body and its passions; we see the rediscovery of the path of humility and charity traced centuries earlier by the Rule of Saint Benedict and so profoundly intuited by the lineage of Cîteaux, which testifies richly to it in the writings of our early Fathers. By following the path of humility and monastic charity we discover the liberating power of filial obedience. We discover the process of conversion dear to Dom Lehodey by which we are transformed through self-giving. We share the discovery that fascinated Mother Pia, of a capacity for offering our lives in love for the Church. For those who are passionate about the monastic way to holiness, a splendid horizon opens out. As

Thomas Merton wrote in 1967, in his "A Letter on the Contemplative Life":

> O my brother, the contemplative is not the man who has
> fiery visions of the cherubim carrying God on their imag-
> ined chariot, but simply he who has risked his mind in
> the desert beyond language and beyond ideas where God
> is encountered in the nakedness of pure trust, that is to
> say in the surrender of our poverty and incompleteness
> in order no longer to clench our minds in a cramp upon
> themselves, as if thinking made us exist. The message of
> hope the contemplative offers you, then, brother, is not that
> you need to find your way through the jungle of language
> and problems that today surround God: but that whether
> you understand or not, God loves you, is present in you,
> lives in you, dwells in you, calls you, saves you, and offers
> you an understanding and light which are like nothing you
> ever found in books or heard in sermons.[14]

Learning from History 2

Cistercian Monasticism in the Second Half of
the Twentieth Century

A number of fundamental changes directed the development of the Order in the second half of the twentieth century. They were in large measure instigated by the prophetic vision of Dom Gabriel Sortais, elected Abbot General of the Order in 1951, who followed in the footsteps of the great figures of prophetic sanctity who left their mark on the first half of the century. Dom Sortais was naturally conditioned by transformations going on in society and culture at the time, yet his vision remained distinctly his own. He was an eager, determined participant in the proceedings of the Second Vatican Council. He followed the first session, which opened on 11 October 1962, in its entirety. During the course of the second session, which lasted from 29 September to 4 December 1963, his life came unexpectedly to an end on 13 November, the feast of All Saints of the Order.

Looking back on those years, it is moving to recall Dom Sortais's relationship with Pope John XXIII. He knew the pope personally and often quoted from his magisterial teaching. Historically speaking, Dom Sortais's shrewd foresight can only partially be said to originate with the Council, but his heart and mind certainly bore the imprint of his careful preparation for that great event in the life of the Church. In a manner of speaking, he was a step ahead of the Council, whose teaching turned out to support and confirm his own vision. The Order's assimilation of Dom Sortais's teaching, meanwhile, was to be radically conditioned by the postconciliar experience, a function of dramatic uncertainty and farsighted provision. These were years that saw the rediscovery of a more thoroughgoing, all-embracing notion of monastic identity that reached beyond the uniformity of the *Usages*, growing out of the new sense of the Church that the Council inspired.

A pleasant modern *apophthegma* that Dom André Louf once shared with me goes some way toward summing up the life of the monk Gabriel Sortais. "A brother asked an elder: 'Who is a monk?' The elder answered, 'He is a monk who asks himself every day: Who is a monk?'" The insights of Dom Sortais were numerous and substantial. They shaped the history of the Order in the second half of the twentieth century. I shall refer only to a limited number of these insights that have been particularly significant in my own life and in the life of my community. Already in his first circular letter to the Order, written on 8 December 1951, Dom Sortais provided a dense summary of his programme of government. His letter began with these words:

> I would like to obtain from God the grace to persuade all members of the Order that they have been called to lead a life of contemplation. For us Cistercians, this is everything. It is by contemplation that we give glory to God. It is by contemplation that we shall become holy. It is by contemplation that we shall help Jesus to save souls.[1]

This contemplative focus informed his entire teaching on monastic observances, which he presented not just as tools of asceticism but as the living format for the contemplative life. Dom Sortais's path was a path of freedom. It referred constantly to the reality of the present time without on that account betraying the purity of the Cistercian charism. Indeed, the charism proved to be open-minded, flexible, and well-grounded as it encountered a new generation:

> *Cistercium mater nostra.* Cîteaux is our mother and we must remain faithful to her. But Cîteaux was born in the twelfth

century, whereas we ascertain that the young men and
women who knock on the doors of our novitiates are not
of the twelfth century. It is an obvious fact. To those who
enter our monasteries we must give the nourishment for
which their souls are hungry, the nourishment they need
to flourish in Cistercian life. [. . .] As for the option of remaining inviolably faithful to a strict observance of very
austere rules, it entails a risk. If, say, we were one day to see
a breakdown in health in the whole Order, would one not
run the risk of becoming extinct for the sake of preserving
certain prescriptions intact, without sufficiently realizing
that this fidelity could probably not be kept except at the
expense of other aspects of monastic life more important,
perhaps, than those one would wish to preserve at all costs?[2]

It was Dom Sortais's insistence on the contemplative nature
of Cistercian life that gave rise to his greatest initiatives of
reform in the Order.

Reforms in Liturgy

Dom Gabriel saw to the simplification of liturgical prayer. He
supervised changes that restored the primacy of the *Opus Dei*,
which had become weighed down by accretions, notably the
Little Office of Our Lady and the Office of the Dead that used
to precede the canonical Hours, reducing the great psalmody
of the *Opus Dei* proper to a rapid recitation *recto tono*. By virtue
of this simplification we gained a new understanding of the
value of the Hours, of the liturgical year, of the content of the
Psalms, of community praise, of the spousal mystery of the
praying Church. The gradual change to a vernacular liturgy
further enriched the process with a creative impetus that, little
by little, attained expressive, artistic, and prayerful maturity.

The new structure of celebration introduced by Vatican II
brought out the significance of the Conventual High Mass as
a single eucharistic celebration that unites the whole community. The devotion of "private masses" (which doubtless
led many a soul to sanctity but did emphasize quantity rather

than quality) receded before a fresh emphasis on the Christian community gathering around the altar as a single assembly. Togetherness was seen to be vitally important. Increasingly, the great eucharistic celebration was understood to be the wellspring from which every other liturgical act draws its sense and value. This insight in turn came to define the liturgical character of the community. We witnessed the slow birth of a sense of ourselves as the people of God, a holy assembly, the communion of the faithful. From this we perceived in a different way, and with urgency, our shared vocation to form the one Body of Christ.

Reforms in Formation

Dom Sortais helped us recover the patrimony of the Cistercian Fathers and a more exact understanding of the doctrine, theology, spirituality, and mysticism of our Fathers. The discovery was at once intellectual and spiritual. It is difficult to gauge the effect of our rereading Saint Bernard, Baldwin of Ford, Aelred, or William of Saint-Thierry (to mention but the most famous) on the formation of a new mentality, a new way of seeing and understanding monastic life. The new generations of sisters were nurtured from the start by a biblical vision, a Cistercian spirituality deriving directly from the experience of Cîteaux. No one will question the importance of correct monastic observance. But whereas a previous age had pursued a style of formation centered on minute details of the *Usages* and *Ritual*, we now came to stress an interiorization of content apt to initiate a process of *conversatio monastica* that sought to be more conscious and deliberate.

Monastic formation as favored by the old observance gave prominence, perhaps, to a degree of moral perfectionism. It exalted physical endurance in the face of penitential austerity and manual labor. It represented a spirituality that cultivated the spirit of sacrifice to the point of immolation. A rigorous experience of humiliation, sustained by the practice of proclamation in the Chapter of Faults, could sometimes exasperate the already frustrating experience of one's own failings. It is certainly true that charity has never ceased to be at the heart of the Cistercian experience of community. Yet in the first years of the twentieth century it seems that our monasteries had not yet awakened to the consciousness of sharing in a single monastic vocation, an insight central to the teaching of Baldwin of Ford. We had lost, somehow, the sense of constituting a communion of calling and grace, of being one in our deliberate, responsible belonging to the shared Cistercian charism that defined the experience of our Fathers.

Our Order has never lost the habit of engaging with the teaching of the Fathers at the level of general spiritual culture. What Dom Gabriel had in mind, however, was something deeper. He wished for a reappraisal of pedagogy and pastoral practice. He wished to develop concrete ways of imparting the *form*, the essential structure of the Cistercian experience, on our life here and now. Hence long periods were once again set aside for *lectio divina*, hence there was a renewed respect for free intervals between times of work. Such adjustments of the timetable gave rise to real battles of interpretation. I have already referred to the importance in my own community of the motto, "Offer yourself up for God." It was seen to express the very highest spirituality, applied to austere observance and hard manual labor, especially in the fields. So strong was this tendency that any attempt to speak up in favor of free intervals for *lectio divina* or study was viewed as a kind of selfish slacking off. True enough, the daily half-hour of *lectio* in common had long been practiced, as we still practice it during Lent. But no guidance or encouragement had been available for personal application to study with a view to penetrating biblical and patristic thought more deeply. With regard to studies, Dom Gabriel had this to say:

> Ignorance, indeed, is always a source of weakness. It engenders error and obstinacy in error. Alternatively, at the

other extreme, it gives rise to a lack of self-confidence that
is prone to make a religious pusillanimous, or to give him a
real inferiority complex. [. . .] The objection could be raised
that by favoring intellectual culture we would develop in
monks a spirit of criticism, or at any rate of independence.
It is true that when we acquire greater knowledge we are
naturally given to compare what we see with what we have
learned. Thus we will tend to exercise our judgment on a
number of problems that a less cultivated intelligence endures without question. But is this a bad thing? Is it the ideal
to make minds anaemic for want of sufficient nourishment,
knowing that they are thus more easily governed? Should
we not rather set out to form minds and cause them to flourish? Should we not have the courage to lead them toward
the sort of maturity that befits an adult, and that we should
not too easily confuse with independence?[3]

In his concern to ensure good formation and to nurture contemplative living, Dom Sortais called quite logically for new
structures. He did not have time to put these fully in place
himself. Nevertheless, his enterprise has left a profound imprint on the development of the Order.

The Unification of the Community

It was Dom Ignace Gillet who, as Abbot General, saw to the
unification of each Cistercian community into a single body.
The process gave rise to challenges we are still faced with
today. At stake was a wish to stress the part played by each
brother, whether choir monk or laybrother, in one and the
same charism within a communion of grace that constitutes
a single Cistercian family. Everyone, we were reminded,
shares in the same vocation, in the same rights and obliga-
tions, though this vocation can be expressed in different ways.

We must not forget the context in which the division between choir monks and laybrothers was debated. At that
point in history we witnessed a real passion for human rights
and human dignity, an eagerness to stress the irreplaceable

contribution each individual was called to make in building society. The formal division between two groups in a single community seemed an anachronism, almost a form of social injustice, though a degree of vocational pluralism was later recognized as an intrinsic value. For those of us who entered monastic life at a young age in the 1950s and 1960s, the differentiation between two classes of nuns seemed unacceptable and absurd. The world we grew up in had been torn apart by warfare and nationalistic hatred. Fundamental values of co-existence had been shattered. Moral and material destruction had been great. Resentment and invincible, absurd rivalries had held sway. What we were hungry for was solidarity. We sought to recognize in one another the same life-giving values, the same faith. We hated divisions, distinctions of class, and agendas of differentiation. We sought a new, truer kind of fraternity. Quite probably, we did not adequately appreciate the ancient charism of the laybrothers and laysisters who had given so much to the Order. We simply could not bear the clear-cut division symbolized by a different habit, a different form of the Divine Office, different work, different criteria for community votes, and so forth. To us, the unification of the two classes of nuns meant pulling down walls of separation within the community, walls that no longer made sense and were apt merely to create negative confrontation and painful frustration. It is likely that this unification carried a quite different resonance in other cultures. For us, however, the recovery of unity within a single vocation (while respecting legitimate diversity) represented a new, invaluable experience of freedom and communion.

The Female Branch of the Order

Under the leadership of Dom Gabriel new attention was given to the female branch of the Order. The nuns were invited to make their specific contribution and to assume greater responsibility. Meetings of abbesses were actively promoted.

The first such, held in 1959, was still rather vaguely defined. Already in 1964, however, the meeting gave proof of vitality and clear purpose. The old *Usages* were at that time still in force, though the process of updating them had begun. With regard to some adaptations of observance emerging in the male branch of Order, the meeting of abbesses adopted a somewhat belligerent position. Nonetheless, progress was made in discussing formation and ways of handing on the Cistercian patrimony to new generations. There was talk of inter-monastic meetings for novice masters and mistresses. The meeting also squarely faced the problems of formation posed by the unification of our communities.

Later, in June 1968, there followed a serious discernment on the stages of monastic initiation. It came to underline the importance of solemn profession as the moment of definitive consecration, whereas the old Cistercian Ritual, following a medieval way of thinking, had tended to ascribe such significance rather to the day of clothing. Ongoing formation was another point on the agenda, and it was asked how the nuns might participate in the government of the Order, how they might find their place within the structure of the Regions. The same meeting of 1968 drafted a *Declaration on Cistercian Life* that was destined to be picked up by the great, charismatic Chapter of 1969. The Chapter reformulated the *Declaration* and in this developed form it marked, alongside the ingenious *Statute on Unity and Pluralism*, the passage of the Order into the reality of a new epoch. It is still useful to recall the original wording of the *Declaration*, which, for all its limitations, constituted a weighty statement:

> The life of the nuns of the Order is based on that sense of God's transcendence that animates the entire Rule and on the centrality given by Saint Benedict to Christ. The nuns who are called to this life respond by seeking God and his will, following the obedient Christ. Purifying her heart by humility, the nun becomes disposed to the pure, continuous prayer that penetrates her day, which is made up of *Opus*

Dei, personal prayer, *lectio divina*, and manual labor. Her way of life is penitential and poor. She lives in an ambience of silence and separation from the world, necessary if she is to dedicate herself entirely to God in contemplation. The nun pursues this search for God in the monastery to which she has vowed her stability. In the charity of Christ, she lives with her sisters in a communion of life under a rule and an abbess. This same charity will make them offer generous Benedictine hospitality. Thus the Cistercian nun desires to correspond fully to the mission entrusted to her by the Church, rendering a magnificent testimony to the majesty and love of God.

It is not difficult to trace here the influence of the encyclical *Venite seorsum*, yet the *Declaration* is not without a depth and originality all its own. This early participation of the nuns in the life of the Order is clearly something we owe to Dom Sortais. Sprung from modest beginnings, it has been constantly enriched over the years. We have become increasingly aware of the necessary complementarity in subsidiarity by which the male and female branches of the Order are integrated in a single whole.

Let us not forget the long way we had to travel in order to obtain the approbation of Rome for our Order's peculiar structure as one entity in two branches with a single Abbot General, a single Abbot General's Council, a joint structure of filiation and Fathers Immediate, and shared General Chapters that were soon organized as Mixed General Meetings. These structures combined to affirm the two branches in a like responsibility for the Cistercian patrimony, for the pastoral care of communities, and for the drawing up of new Constitutions for the Order.

The Missionary Dimension of Cistercian Life

We recognize another aspect of Dom Sortais's heritage in the prophetic impetus he provided for the Order's missionary outreach. Already in 1961, in a conference held at Ligugé, he spoke as follows:

[I should like] to insist on the duty now incumbent on monks
to make foundations, whenever they can, in mission territories. That such a duty exists cannot be doubted by anyone
who remembers what Pope Pius XI wrote to the Apostolic
Prefects and Vicars in 1926: "We insistently exhort the Superiors General of contemplative Orders to introduce and
ever more to spread this form of more austere life in mission
territories by founding monasteries." [. . .] The sons of Saint
Benedict have a long tradition of fidelity to the Holy See, of
striving to correspond to its thinking. An invitation so clearly
expressed amounts to an order as far as we are concerned.
There is no need for further arguments to persuade us of the
need to make monastic foundations in mission territories.[4]

He insisted that the call to transmit monastic life to new
countries and cultures was not to be regarded as an *option* by
contemporary monks: "It imposes itself as a demand intrinsic to the nature of monasticism, as soon as we realize how
closely the nature of monasticism is related to the nature of
the Church."[5] It was during Dom Sortais's tenure as Abbot
General that we saw the generous expansion of Cistercian
monasticism on the African continent, mainly from French
and English houses, while the American monasteries looked
south toward Latin America. In 1967 and 1968 Dom Edmund
Futterer and Dom Augustin Roberts drew up a first account
of the situation in Latin America, which until then had been
all but excluded from the missionary expansion of the Order,
with the notable exception of Spencer's efforts to found the
Argentinian monastery of Azul in 1958, and two years later
to set up the community of La Dehesa in Chile.

Today, as members of an abundantly international, intercul-
tural Order, we can easily forget the great labor required just
after the Second World War to ensure a missionary outreach
for the Order. Certainly, there has never been an absence of
missionary energy in an Order that from its earliest beginnings knew a phenomenal monastic expansion. Nor should
we forget the foundations made already at the end of the

nineteenth century. The Chinese monastery of Consolation
was established in 1883. Latroun, in Israel, followed in 1890.
Our Lady of the Lighthouse began life in 1896, while two years
later, through the joint effort of Ubexy and Laval, Cistercian
nuns, too, reached Japan to found the monastery of Tenshien.
Thus began the Japanese monastic expansion, which has since
borne abundant fruit. The mid-twentieth century likewise
saw a handful of foundations. Rawaseneng in Indonesia was
founded by Tilburg in 1953, only eight years after the end of
the War. In 1956 the same motherhouse sent a group of founders to Victoria in Kenya. The Irish abbey of Roscrea gave birth
to Tarrawarra in Australia in 1954; Mont-des-Cats founded
Maromby in Madagascar in 1958. The missionary expansion
had, then, been operative for quite some time when Dom
Sortais, once in office, considerably magnified its potential.

We recognize the effect of this expansion on the Order as a
whole. It fostered a new mentality that was more universal,
more ecclesial. Through the challenges raised by inculturation
and adaptation, an essential part of the Cistercian patrimony
was recovered and freed from a cultural superstructure that
had arisen through the Order's immersion in an exclusively
European context.

On this note I conclude my reflection on the great riches bestowed on the Order by Dom Sortais, a contribution that merits
attention precisely on account of its influence on twentieth-
century monasticism. We have reason to be grateful to Dom
Sortais for facing a crucial moment in the history of mankind,
of the Church, and of the Order. In the midst of many contradictions and much hard work he was able to communicate his
unswerving hope and his faith in the future of monasticism.

1969: A Salient Moment in Our History

The balance of the Order was shaken in many ways at the beginning of the second half of the twentieth century. The challenges faced were various: the extraordinary rate of historical
and social change in the world at large; the arrival in our

monasteries of a new generation carrying a different cultural baggage and a spiritual, social, and ecclesial sensibility that often did not match that of previous generations; the Order's ever greater missionary expansion. Each monastery made its own discoveries, changes, and experiences. Each community grew in its own particular way. So great was the experimentation that characterized the years from 1967 to 1969 that the very unity and identity of the Order seemed to be at stake.

There is wide agreement in considering the famous General Chapter of 1969 to have been especially charismatic. It rediscovered the values and substance that would safeguard the imperiled unity of the Order. In this it gave proof of unrivaled perspicacity. The Chapter's deliberations resulted in two acclaimed documents, the *Declaration on Cistercian Life* and the *Statute on Unity and Pluralism*. These were to form the basis of the Order's subsequent development and of its new Constitutions. The notion of unity advocated from now on no longer presupposed a precise uniformity of usages and customs. It called, rather, for a responsible, faithful recognition of the values that define who we are, admitting that this grace may assume different expressions in different cultural circumstances.

New Challenges

In the wake of that luminous moment in 1969, the Order witnessed a great deal of experimentation inspired by current tendencies in Western society. By way of example I shall touch briefly on three such influences: the culture of psychoanalysis (especially in Europe); the influence of the great Eastern religions (especially in the United States); and the impact of liberation theology (especially in Latin America).

The Culture of Psychoanalysis

No one will question the precious contribution made by psychological and psychoanalytical research in increasing our understanding of the depths of the unconscious. These disciplines can reveal much about the mechanisms of behavior and relationship. Problems arise, however, when insights of this kind are made the sole criterion of monastic discernment and formation. The pedagogical balance proper to monastic life is upset, while the standards of monastic conversion are displaced from the realm of the Gospel and the Rule to that of analysis and psychological accompaniment. This implies a shift in focus from God to self. Faith-filled reference to authority is compromised; the coenobitic common life is robbed of its trans-forming, sanctifying force insofar as communities so affected tend to lose a sense of their sacramental nature, of the freeing force exercised by a constant search for the common good and by experiences of mutual forgiveness and daily reconciliation.

I recall how in some monastic circles it was said at that time: "The community does not exist; only persons exist," as if there were a contradiction between "person" and "com-munity." This line of reasoning supposes that well-formed, mature, deliberately minded persons will necessarily create a solid, grown-up community. There was a tendency to con-sider a person's growth apart from the formative, sanctifying crucible of the common life. The community then acquired a status that was purely sociological, which to all intents and purposes excluded the sacramental, ecclesial mystery of the Benedictine *coenobium*.

Not long ago, I was pleasantly surprised to find, in the re-ports of the Regional Conferences from 1995, a simple, sane re-covery of obviously monastic values. The Region of the United States, for instance, put the community back on the agenda as an environment of growth and healing for the person, the per-son who today is wounded by the epidemic anguish caused by the affective breakup of family life, the loss of subjective identity, and a sense of futility. The Spanish Region devoted much space to reviewing the role and service of authority. The Latin American Region affirmed that teaching in the "school of charity" must be guided by the indications of Saint Benedict's twelve steps of humility. The report of the Italian Region made the point that our coenobitic experience far surpasses mere tolerance; rather, it constitutes a living environment of mutual help in which we discover our particular grace as well as that of each brother or sister, with all of us together assuming the identity of the community. It follows from this evaluation that a clear vocational criterion is our capacity to enter into the identity of our particular community while remaining, naturally, fully ourselves.

I was struck by a vigorous return to the certainty that personal growth and the development of a monastic vocation cannot happen apart from the educational, healing role of the community; that it presupposes paternal or maternal authority as the wellspring of sonship; that it must follow the proven path of monastic conversion and Benedictine humility. Thus a long process of searching and experimentation may be seen to culminate in a splendid reappraisal of a monastic tradition that *can* take on board the insights of psychological science without on that account relinquishing the living wisdom that is peculiarly its own.

The Influence of Eastern Religious Traditions

Many of our contemporaries engage in an earnest search for spirituality while rejecting organized religion. Every form of organized Christianity (Protestant as well as Catholic) has of late found that the number of ordained ministers is falling and that the religious practice of the faithful is decreasing. It is often said that the drop in Catholic priestly vocations is caused by the requirement of celibacy. The faithful, it is argued, are drawn away by contemporary atheistic, hedonistic trends. It would seem that the real reasons go deeper. They point to the difficulties involved in taking on a permanent commitment, of opening the doors wide to faith in Christ. In a climate of moral and religious relativism, it is hard to adopt religious faith as a structuring element of life. We often see how men and women, when faced with this challenge, engage instead in a strange search for the unpredictable and miraculous. They reach out for some cosmic energy of dubious spiritual status that offers to carry them beyond the limits of what is merely earthly, promising a transcendence that will relieve them of their humdrum human reality. Within this context, the Eastern religions seem to offer an attractive tonic to tired modern man, proposing ascetic discipline and concentration as well as a path toward mastery of the passions and emotions. Often, the fundamental motivation behind this attraction is good. The Eastern religions' disciplinary rigor merits our esteem; so does their search for methods of meditation and sublimation. However, man cannot attain to authentic sublimation as long as he remains at the center of his own spiritual experiment, whether it is conceived of as the confluence of cosmic energy or as the abyssal descent to the heart of our own vital energy. In a Christian perspective, the human person can reach the fullness of his or her vocation only in the encounter with Jesus Christ, the sole author of life and redemption. It is an encounter that the Holy Spirit can bring about even apart from conscious acceptance of the Christian faith. Where this encounter does not take place, however, what occurs is nothing but a confrontation with ourselves as we painfully crash against our ontological boundary, our own existential anguish. No *nirvana* culminates in love or is bathed in the loving fullness of the Father's divine otherness.

The fascination exerted by Eastern religion has been great nonetheless. For a time, there was talk in Christian monastic circles of embracing a range of spiritual techniques such as yoga, zen, transcendental meditation, or the employment of a mantra. Yet one can hardly be initiated into such techniques without at the same time assimilating the philosophy from which they flow. The individualism generated by such practices comes to the fore. Communities that go this way eventually disintegrate for want of a common spirit. Authority is valued only insofar as it presents a specific charismatic quality. As a result, the crucial encounter with Christ and the Gospel is relativized, even thwarted.

At the basis of these tendencies there seems to me to be a lack of hope. In this connection I will now consider Joseph Ratzinger's argument in his book *To Look on Christ*, specifically in the chapter on "Hope and Love," even though this work does not make explicit reference to spiritual experience inspired by the Eastern tradition. According to Ratzinger, the loss of hope gives birth to two forms of response that appear to be opposed and yet are in fact related. They are despair and temerity:

> According to [Thomas Aquinas] the root of despair is to be found in what has been termed acidie: for want of a better word, we usually translate this as sloth or inertia, by which very much more, and something deeper, is meant than mere idleness, than lacking the inclination to be active. According to Thomas this metaphysical inertia is identical with the "sorrow of the world," the "worldly grief" of which Paul says that it produces death (2 Corinthians 7:10).[6]

And men and women unaware of their metaphysical grandeur cannot be realists:

> Today there is a remarkable hatred among people for their own real greatness. Man sees himself as the enemy of life, of the balance of creation, as the great disturber of the peace of nature (which would be better off if he did not exist), as the creature that went wrong. His salvation and the salvation of the world would on this view consist of his disappearing, of his life and soul being taken back from him, of what is specifically human vanishing so that nature could return to its unconscious perfection in its own rhythm and with its own wisdom of dying and coming into being. At the start of the road stood the pride of wanting to "be like God." We had to shake off the Big Brother God who is spying on us in order to be free, take back into ourselves the God projected into the heavens and ourselves rule over creation as God. Thus there arose in fact a kind of spirit and will that was and is opposed to life and is a dominion of death. The more perceptible this becomes the more the original intention turns into its opposite while remaining trapped in the same point of departure: man—who only wanted to be his own

creator and to reassemble creation himself; with *Acedia* is a
lack of magnanimity. It makes us blind to the grandeur of
man and to the immensity of a better form of evolution he
had thought out himself—this man ends in self-negation
and self-destruction. He finds it would be better if he were
not there.[7]

This kind of *acedia* is the sister of despair and presumption.
It produces what Ratzinger calls a "bourgeois liberal Pela-
gianism" that says to itself, "If God really does exist and if
he does in fact bother about people, he cannot be so fear-
fully demanding as is described by the faith of the Church."
Ratzinger retorts: "Perhaps in times of peace one can live for
quite a long time in this frame of mind. But at the moment
of crisis people will either be converted from it or fall victim
to despair."[8]

With such an outlook we confine ourselves to seeking a
bourgeois kind of self-satisfaction that precludes the experience of forgiveness. It presupposes the inevitability of conflict and so looks for an arrangement of accommodation that
may display tolerance but is deprived of hope. For it does
not aspire to integrate conflict in an authentic experience of
peace and reconciliation. It looks for no more than an apparent security.

As long as they uphold an entitlement to contentment, we
may reach the point of accepting norms that constrain social
behavior. We do not, however, set out on the path of truth
in humility. We do not run the supreme risk of love. In his
Apostolic Letter *Tertio millennio adveniente*, Saint John Paul II
presented the absolute novelty of the Christ-event for the men
and women of today. He said:

> The religion founded upon Jesus Christ is a *religion of glory*;
> it is a newness of life for the praise of the glory of God (cf.
> Ephesians 1:12). All creation is in reality a manifestation of
> his glory. In particular, man [*vivens homo*] is the epiphany
> of God's glory, man who is called to live by the fullness of
> life in God. (*Tertio millennio adveniente*, n. 6)

The Influence of Liberation Theology

Although we may not always register it, liberation theology has had a major impact on the Church at large. It has even exerted a certain influence in monastic circles. We currently witness a rediscovery of the positive insight of this theology. Freed from the violent aspect of revolutionary opposition, it carries a profound yearning for social justice and for the liberation of man from every form of moral and material enslavement. In its confused beginnings, liberation theology may have led some communities to interpret the communion of the Church with a sociological slant, democratizing to an unreasonable extent the government of the common life by, for instance, submitting every decision to the approval of all the members and by reducing the service of authority to mere facilitation, shorn of any mandate to decide. At one General Chapter, I recall, the report of a community voting to determine the color of an item of furniture attracted attention.

Liberation theology makes much of the famous "option for the poor." It is a self-evident, noble Gospel value. In some contexts, however, this option has displaced the primary focus of Christian living from the preaching of the Gospel to an engagement with social justice that sometimes carries a polemic edge. As a result, this engagement no longer carries authentically religious content. It is easy to see how excessive stress on sociological and democratic factors causes the value of religious obedience to erode. Meanwhile, in this perspective, the experience of mutual forgiveness will probably no longer be considered an indispensable element of peace in the community. A dynamic of subjective rights upheld and imposed may cause the erosion of that Benedictine solidarity that pursues mutual service and a loving acceptance of each brother.

An Epoch-Making Document

In 1971, the Order produced a document titled *From a Community of Observance to a Community of Consensus*. It seems that this text has often passed unnoticed. Its influence has nevertheless been very great. A quarter of a century after it was issued, while I was attending the Regional Conference of Latin America in 1996, it surprised me to hear the very same formula, "From a Community of Observance to a Community of Consensus," used repeatedly, with ready acknowledgment of the consequences on formation and teaching it involved. The aim at that conference of 1996 was to facilitate three values: the attainment of a common vision, the growth of the community as a school of charity, and the search for the common good through dialogue.

The 1971 document, in fact, did much to modify the mentality, even the structure, of our communities. Little by little, they moved from a perfect uniformity of observance founded on the *Usages* toward the loving search for a consensus of hearts and minds. The goal has been to ensure that each person is responsibly involved in the life and progress of his or her community. Discernment is no longer understood superficially, as a judgment of an individual's outward behavior or performance at work. Rather, each brother or sister is accepted with cordial sincerity, and an effort is made to apply discernment to their value as a person, without focusing too much on perfection in small details. We have come to see that the way in which a monk or nun responds to the grace of the Order and the house is more important than minute fidelity to customs and traditions. Together, as a community, we strive to foster trust and freedom, obedience and belonging, mutual fidelity and a capacity for friendship. In short, we strive to live together in such a way that we together build up the monastic Church.

In 1973 or thereabout my community was beginning to articulate the values of obedience and communion in the terms just described. I recall how we found it very hard to get our point across at a particular General Chapter. We were accused of favoring an obedience that was blind and irresponsible, of wanting to cast all the nuns, especially the youngest, in a single mold. What we were in fact saying was the opposite. For us, to speak of obedience and communion was basically to speak of freedom and responsibility, respect and friendship, belonging and creativity. Perhaps our shared intuition was still premature at the time. Still, I remember how, at the Chapter, the old abbot of Bricquebec, Dom Joseph-Marie, stood up and responded with insight and kindness. He told the assembly: "More than anything else, the young who enter our monasteries today need fathers and mothers, guides who can teach them to discover obedience as a path of freedom." At that moment, we felt as if we had just passed a difficult exam.

What was really at stake was the application to our communities of the Vatican Council's ecclesiology of communion that today we take for granted as the cornerstone of the monastic community. In the early seventies, however, such application was no easy matter, exposed as it was to a tension between destructive democratization, on the one hand, and fearful conservatism, on the other. While this transformation was taking place at the level of individual communities, the Order as a whole, too, took on board the values of communion. It spelled them out in terms of "collegiality" and the "bond of charity." The search for unity and cooperation in the Regions began as an attempt to give each house a share in joint pastoral responsibility for the Order. The same purpose was served by cultural and formative exchanges between monasteries. We all sought to affirm our belonging to a shared Cistercian charism in a deliberate way. The effort to foster communion found expression in the drawing up of our new *Constitutions*, of the *Ratio studiorum* on initial and ongoing formation, and in a handful of new statutes.

Some notable figures were meanwhile providing vital impulses for the Order. I shall never forget my first impression of Dom Ambrose Southey, elected Abbot General in 1974. I saw a man who assumed the responsibilities entrusted to him in the first person, positive, decided, and vigorously clear-sighted. One of Dom Ambrose's qualities that soon became proverbial was his rare ability to put problems on the table resolutely and as a matter of fact, without subterfuge and without holding anything back. Having reached that point, he would make a sincere judgment that affirmed the strength of the positive while straightforwardly unmasking the negative. His paternal care to sustain and support our communities on their path of conversion was unfailing.

As regards Dom Bernardo Olivera, Abbot General from 1990 to 2008, we all know the lucid, synthetic clarity that characterizes his judgment, nurtured by a contemplative spirit and phenomenal foresight. Whereas Dom Ambrose saw to the immense work of drawing up the Constitutions, it was Dom Bernardo who assumed the task of applying them without compromise or contradiction. At the end of the twentieth century, the Order of Cistercians of the Strict Observance stands out as singular, exceptional presence in the Church. This is so for several reasons. We may mention the Order's explicitly monastic identity that is at once contemplative and coenobitic; its joint structure of two branches that are not simply parallel but adapted one to the other in respect for autonomy and difference; its commitment to formation and to finding effective ways of passing on the Cistercian heritage; the originality inherent in the structure of filiations; the heartfelt mutual interest and responsibility that exists among the houses of the Order; the strength of its missionary expansion; and finally, the incalculably precious testimony of its communities of martyrs. All this gives the Order a stature in the Church that is far from insignificant. However, as at every stage of history, what matters most is what is most essential: our God-given vocation to follow the path of humility outlined by the Rule of Saint Benedict many centuries ago, letting humility, obedience, mutual charity, and continuous praise fill time and space with fraternal communion in response to the Word of God.

The Vision of the Church

The Church I would put into words is
My *Church, born with me,*
But not about to die with me, nor will I die
With her that ever surpasses me;
The Church, wellspring and summit of my being;
The Church, whose roots embrace both past and future,
The Sacrament of my being in God, my Father.
      —*Karol Wojtyła,* Stanislaus

Vitorchiano's passion for the Church is not a recent development. Already many years ago, thanks to the ecumenical impetus of Mother Pia Gullini, we began to assimilate this passion in its widest dimensions. We let it penetrate our consciousness. It goes without saying that a sense of the Church, what we like to call an *ecclesial awareness*, is fundamental to a community entirely structured by the praise of the Lord, whose rhythm of time, work, and common life is defined by the celebration of the Liturgy of the Hours. A community that understands itself fundamentally as a place of prayer for the salvation of the world cannot but be keenly aware of the Church.

Our sense of the Church matured progressively in the wake of the Second World War, thanks to the new generations that continued to flock to our monastery. The war years had caused the collapse of many high ideals, ideals of humanity, civic life, patriotism, national unity, and human dignity. For many it was

crucial to discover that the Church, and she alone, had come
through the trauma strong in her faith, holy in her martyrs.
Church-run youth movements were able at last to emerge
from the sacristy and into the open, after years of oppression
by the dominant political regime. For many young people,
membership in such movements entailed a rediscovery of
dignity and enthusiasm, a reclaiming of youth. They discovered something of the meaning of life and developed a zest
for it. The Church, the pope, the Catholic youth group: these
were vital points of reference at that time, enabling hope to
rise anew from the rubble of an aberrant war.

For all its austerity and separation from the world, our monastery could not remain unaffected by these currents. They
informed a new sensibility and provided a new perspective on
the historical reality in which we were immersed. Meanwhile,
the typical features of the Benedictine-Cistercian experience
exercised a powerful attraction on young people whom the
war had left values-less and deprived of a destiny. Carrying
the wounds of destruction, they were drawn by the grandeur of liturgical prayer, by the strength derived from living
together in community, by the poverty that calls for earnest
manual labor in our effort to earn our daily bread, by a life
entirely built on the certainty of having a destiny that reaches
out toward eternal life.

The young were looking for meaning. They sought imper-
ishable values. They desired a Beyond solid enough to with-
stand the burning of time. They longed to follow an authority
that would not betray them. For many, the sum total of all
this had a name; it was *the Church*. The life-giving experience
of the Church involved the discovery of a new dimension of
humanity, recognized as forming *the people of God*. The experience engendered many religious vocations. A number
of young women presented themselves at the doors of our
monastery, which they found to correspond to their thirst for
meaning. The ecclesial awareness I am referring to was still
embryonic, awaiting the immeasurably broad vision of the

Second Vatican Council. Still, it had all the strength of long-sustained pain and passionate seeking.

It was the Council, obviously, that provided us with a formidable body of teaching on the mystery of the Church as proceeding from the Father in the redemptive blood of the Son by the work of the Holy Spirit. The Council taught us to see the Church as a sign and sacrament of humanity's union with God, as the new Israel, as the people of the new Covenant, as the bride of Christ and his mystical Body. The Church, we learned, embodies our eschatological hope and constitutes the way to the fullness of truth about man, about time, about life itself. The Church is holy, constantly unified by the Holy Spirit "in communion and in works of ministry" (*Lumen gentium*, 4).

These two terms, "communion" and "ministry," soon became part of a common vocabulary. They rendered the Greek terms *koinonia* and *diakonia* and expressed the especial insight of Vatican II. Underlying the notion of *koinonia* is an understanding of the Church *as* communion, that is, as an intimate, real, life-giving participation in the mystery of Christ, a sharing in his passion, resurrection, and glory. As *koinonia* the Church conforms us to the sonship of Christ that, as a ripe fruit, engenders communion among ourselves in fraternity and concord. Hearts and minds are united. We learn to work together and to share in one another's lives. These notions quickly entered the core of Cistercian vocabulary in the 1970s and 1980s.

From the dogmatic constitution *Lumen gentium* we learned to regard the Church as a messianic people that has Christ for its head, founded on the dignity and freedom of the sons of God in whose hearts the Holy Spirit dwells as in a temple, a people bound for the Kingdom of God inaugurated on earth by God himself, destined to reach the ends of the earth so as to be the instrument of universal redemption. The Spirit gathers together in communion, in *koinonia*, those who look to Jesus Christ with faith. He fashions them into the Church, into an operative principle of communion, unity, and peace. We derive our ecclesial awareness from the pledge of the Holy Spirit, who models our will to seek oneness and conversion.

The Church, then, is communion. It is the messianic people, the sacrament of salvation. Alongside these insights, the Council made us acutely aware of the Church's concern for man, for humankind. It is an emphasis we find repeated throughout the catechesis of Pope John Paul II. To remain within the family, as it were, we may also cite Dom John Eudes Bamberger, the former abbot of Genesee in upstate New York, who in 1968 spoke of the philanthropic concern that had been present at every stage and every level of the Council, underpinned by the Council's new anthropological vision:

> Vatican II tells us that man is a being in dialogue, someone who does not know who he is until another reveals it to him. For man is that being to whom God speaks. By speaking, God reveals not only his own Being to man; in a real way, he also reveals man to himself. [. . .] Finally, a series of statements in the Council documents testifies to an acute awareness of man as essentially a social being. The social dimension is not something that is added to his being. It belongs integrally to the structure of his being.

Having drawn out the significance of this insight, Dom John Eudes makes a weighty conclusion of his own:

> Our interior world is in the image of the world that sur-rounds us, our social world, for the self only develops in interaction with various organized forms of social activity. [. . .] Considering this fact we discover, I think, why the styles and structures of the community are so important for the spiritual life: they determine our true identity much more than we are inclined to suppose. It is not only that other people and social environment influence us; they re-fashion us.[1]

A recurrent theme at General Chapters in the late 1960s was this: the community is not somehow juxtaposed to the individuals that constitute it; it is not just a function of rules and regulations. No, the community is a living body that makes choices. It must invest the communion it aims for, the vocation that defines it, with solidity and authenticity.

The process by which we came to assimilate this vision, this concern for the Church, was intense. It helped us elaborate an explicitly ecclesial pedagogy that would animate our program of monastic formation as its predominant, most efficaciously constructive aspect. In what way has our ecclesial vision and our pedagogy of communion had a concrete impact on our life? How have we endeavored to remain faithful? Insofar as we invest the notion of fidelity with an ecclesial dimension, we must go beyond a concern merely for the perfect execution of observances and usages; we must pay responsible attention to the magisterium of the Church and of the Order, the magisterium of tradition, and the magisterium of our community. We must listen to the magisterium of the superior and seniors while learning from the insights of the young. We must be susceptible to the authoritative wisdom that is implicit in the particular grace of our own house and of its history.

The Magisterium of the Church

First of all I should like to cite from an address by Cardinal Angelo Sodano to the Synod on Consecrated Life in 1994. I find it provides a useful key as we try to understand what is implicit in the phrase, *sentire cum Ecclesia*:

> The obligation to remain united to the Church's pastors is incumbent on all the faithful, but it especially concerns those who have made a vow of obedience in the Church. [. . .] True enough, our understanding of what it means to *sentire cum Ecclesia* may vary. However, the essential content must always remain intact, today as yesterday. For any religious, *sentire cum Ecclesia* must always mean *cogitare cum Ecclesia, iudicare cum Ecclesia, criteria habere quae Ecclesia habet.* [. . .] In one of his rules for *sentire cum Ecclesia*, Saint

> Ignatius writes that it is unthinkable to criticize the Church,
> for the Church is our Mother. The Church cannot be judged,
> for she is the Spouse of Christ. [. . .] *Sentire cum Ecclesia* is
> thus transformed into *amare Ecclesiam*, just as Christ loved
> the Church and gave himself up for her in order to make
> her holy, without spot or wrinkle (cf. Eph 5:25-27) . [. . .]
> The Church, it is true, is *semper reformanda*. It is no less true
> that the reform must begin with each one of us.[2]

I use this quotation as often as I can. I sense that it expresses
our community's experience and particular pedagogy, not
only with reference to the universal Church, but also with
reference to the small local Church that is constituted by our
community.

We apply the principle of *sentire cum Ecclesia* to our own
pedagogy by giving careful attention to pontifical documents.
We study them, discuss them, and keep them as a constant
point of reference in formation. The pope remains a prophetic
figure, with a mandate to interpret life and history. One way in
which we express our familiar, affectionate fidelity is by listening, whenever possible, to his *Angelus* addresses on Sundays.
The great messages of Easter and Christmas provide the only
occasions during the year on which we watch direct televi-
sion. We further have the splendid tradition of never sending
off a group of foundresses to their destination without first
receiving the pope's blessing in an audience. The foundresses
carry this blessing with them as a mandate and *viaticum* for
the new life about to begin. A particularly significant moment
in our history was an encounter with Pope Paul VI by the
foundresses setting off for Argentina in 1973. The meeting was
special because the foundation was our first venture overseas.
It was special, too, because of the dialogue that developed
between the nuns and the by then elderly pope, whose face
was furrowed by pain and anxiety for the Church. Suddenly,
his face radiated a special intensity. His eyes, though sunk
into their orbits, flashed with a remarkably lively, personal
attention. "What are you going to Latin America to do?" he

asked. "You are going to that continent to pray in it and for it. Standing on its soil, you assume it within your vocation. You are going there to pray there." We felt it clearly: the emphatic "there" was a mandate from the Church that indicated our destiny.

Another milestone in the unfolding of our ecclesial awareness was the beatification of Sister Maria Gabriella in 1983. It was not just that we rejoiced in having one of our sisters recognized a saint; not just that the occasion involved our community in far-reaching ecumenical relations. What mattered most to us was the way in which the Church, tenderly yet solemnly, bowed before one of its "little ones," holding our sister up as a model of Christian sanctity. We saw the Church recognizing its mystery as being somehow condensed in Sister Maria Gabriella's brief life. It drew out the significance of what it had seen and stamped it with a seal of recognition. In no way had we aimed to obtain such recognition, nor should we have been able to pursue it without the able, efficient help of the Order's Postulator for the Causes of Saints, Father Paolino Beltrame Quattrocchi. In no way do we consider it a source of pride. It is true, though, that the beatification represented an especially intense encounter with Mother Church as she recognized, at the heart of the poor community of Grottaferrata, an example of humble sanctity, of genuine conversion, of fidelity to God's call, of an authentic desire to perform an oblation in order that the Church might live. Events such as these entered the flow of a living process and exerted a powerful influence on our effort to articulate a pedagogy of monastic formation.

The Magisterium of Tradition

One grace characteristic of our community resides in the lowliness of our origins. We cannot boast of any kind of glorious beginning, nor of charismatic and effective initial growth. No, there was none of this when Mother Thérèse Astoin set out in obscurity to head the foundation made by the community

of Vaise at San Vito near Turin. Perhaps it is precisely on account of these poor beginnings that we can find in our tradition
a real school of humility and charity. It flourished wonderfully in the first generations that lived first at San Vito, then
at Grottaferrata.

Our Menology is significant in this respect, offering abundant pickings of *fioretti* that are rich in interest and demon-
strate an attitude of humility so widespread that it seems
(as indeed it was) to have been taken for granted. Now, the
attitudes that are taken for granted in any community will
always reveal something about a certain style of formation, of
pedagogy in action. It is worthwhile, therefore, to recall some
of these *fioretti* as they occur in the Menology. They point to
a magisterium of tradition that we should not forget, for in
it we find striking examples of charity, humility, fidelity to
superiors, abandonment to God, and great faith. Consider
the following examples:

> Sister Gerarda (1877–1904) was among the first postulants of
> Grottaferrata. She did not perform any outstanding works
> but observed the Rule and obedience in the best possible
> way. The common life brought her to perfection. She lived
> in our midst without attracting attention.

> Sister Giuseppina (1876–1904) considered herself the least
> of all and suffered when subject to the attention of others.
> Her customary motto was: "All for God! To God we can
> never say: Enough!" Her life here below did not last long.
> She lived the religious life for no more than seven years,
> but they were full years. She died as she had lived, smiling,
> happy, fully given over to God. Her only complaint was that
> she was treated too well.

> Sister Geltrude (1853–1907) would run to Mother Abbess
> to unburden herself of anything that weighed her down.
> Having received a good scolding from the abbess, her peace
> was restored. As soon as troublesome thoughts returned, she
> would come along again, begging the abbess to scold her, for
> this, she said, was the best way of "clearing up her head."

Sister Domitilla (1883–1909) would be the first to arrive in choir, which she sustained with her lovely voice. She was the first, too, to arrive at work, where she gave of herself with all the ardor of her youth. She was exact in community exercises. Profoundly devoted to her superiors, she would execute any order without delay. Don Ignazio used to refer to her as the community's "little bird."

Sister Zaccaria (1848–1917) found all the sisters edifying, holding all in great esteem. She was always prompt to serve, to render a favor, and to help. She was as indifferent to heat as to cold, to the rain as to the wind. Although she was illiterate and a person of immense simplicity, she must have received some special insight regarding a phrase from the liturgy: *O admirabile commercium.* She repeated it with special delight, in season and out of season. Spade in hand, she would sometimes freeze into immobility and exclaim, with rapt attention, *O admirabile commercium!*

Sister Clementina (1885–1918) once, on an evening in winter, received a vigorous rebuke from the abbess while standing in the kitchen. Following the usage then in force, Sister Clementina prostrated herself on the ground while the abbess hurried on to other things, quite unaware of leaving the poor sister prostrate on the floor. It was already late when the abbess returned to the kitchen on some other errand and stumbled over Sister Clementina who was still lying prostrate, awaiting the command to rise.

Through this magisterium of tradition we can learn to acquire a *sensus Ecclesiae.* We note a moving fidelity to superiors, motivated by sincere affection and unshakable trust in the power of a superior's word to heal and liberate. From this results an obedience of great simplicity. Its manifestations may strike us as naïve, though when put to the test this obedience proves to be so radical, so convinced and convincing, that it is worthy of paradigmatic status. We further note essential features of relationships within the community. The sisters looked up to one another and were generous in helping one another. They found deep contentment in what the community could offer

them. With simple, strong gestures of real dedication they con-
cretely displayed their sense of belonging. Dedication of this
kind is driven spontaneously, by virtue of an inner logic, to
flower in humility. Today we are struck by the parallels between
this fundamental attitude and the passion for humility that
defines John Paul II's apostolic letter *Tertio millennio adveniente*
in which the pope gave voice to the "joy of conversion" in a
humble plea for forgiveness.

The very great poverty of our origins has left an essential imprint on every level of our community's experience,
whether at San Vito, Grottaferrata, or Vitorchiano. In the magisterium of our particular tradition, the experience of poverty
is a cornerstone. We recognize it in our foundations too, if not
in a poverty of origins, then in their many initial failures on
the path of conversion. This magisterium has allowed our
community to find its place quite naturally in the school of
humility; of this I am convinced. In this school we learn a
charity that is eager to serve. We learn to be thankful for every
little gift received, for gratitude is the seal of our belonging.
This school teaches an affectionate, listening fidelity to our
superiors. Thus it gives birth to a real pedagogy, profoundly
rooted in the Church.

At the Synod for Consecrated Life, Cardinal Sodano recalled
the practical implications of *sentire cum Ecclesia*. It involves
*cogitare cum Ecclesia, iudicare cum Ecclesia, criteria habere quae
Ecclesia habet*: "thinking with the Church, judging with the
Church, having the criteria that the Church has." We can see, I
think, that this has informed the magisterium of our particular
tradition and the monastic pedagogy that has formed entire
generations of nuns. Obviously, we have at times stumbled off
course through infidelity, weakness, and weariness. However,
something of this strong *sensus Ecclesia* has survived to this
day. It remains with us and enables us to carry on absorbing
and enriching the tradition that has given us life.

The Magisterium of Authority

Intrinsic to our pedagogy of formation, the notion of authority that defines the features of our house has always been understood in terms of life-giving maternity. The abbess is the mother who brings us to life in Christ, with whose help our life is directed and shaped. Luigi Giussani, a prophetic figure of our times, once remarked that

> It is not by learning or applying criteria and ideas that we become obedient. Obedience consists in looking continuously toward someone who is bringing you to life. Someone who is a disciple may learn and repeat a given script, being presumptuous enough, perhaps, to interpret it in his own way. Someone who is a son, on the other hand, continuously receives life from his father. This life he, in turn, passes on.[3]

Life itself teaches us that we cannot become fully adult unless we receive life from a father, from a mother. Without such transmission we do not enter the fullness of life, we do not receive the imprint of that creative, unrepeatable seal that shapes our identity. In the context of monastic life, we do not, without a mother or father, receive the *forma Christi* that is at the heart of our vocation, expressing the special grace and charism of our community. Only if we let ourselves be brought to life in this way do we enter the land of reality, freed of illusions. Only in this way do we discover a freedom that is not simply autonomy, a gratuity that is not passive, a sense of responsibility that is not authoritarian but rather founded on service. Only in this way do I receive what I need in order to truly become an adult, in order to truly become a *son*. People who have never had this formative, life-giving experience (or who have refused it by dictate of an absurd autonomy, ultimately a refusal to live) typically remain arrested in a dynamic of pretentious childishness, ever manipulated by mechanisms of confrontation and frustration.

In the monastic pedagogy we have received, special weight has always been given to the teaching of the community's

Mother, that is, of the abbess. We have learned to consider her teaching as a life-giving word for the community as a whole and for the life of each sister. From her word, our monastery's *sensus Ecclesiae* is born. By listening to it, we learn to "think with the Church, judge with the Church, have the criteria that the Church has." We cannot invent the ecclesial dimension of our life, of our own heart, from scratch. We need to listen with humility and perseverance. We need to will to learn and to examine ourselves. The transparency required in order to receive what is held out to us can never be taken for granted. There always lurks the risk that we will use authority as a tool to obtain what *we* feel we need, what *we* hold dear, what *we* consider appropriate.

The Magisterium of the Community

The magisterium of the community is born from the awareness that the community is God's dwelling place, the place where the Spirit speaks to the Church. It is in this place that the solidity of my vocation and of my very identity as a person is put to the test. At the Synod on Consecrated Life, Cardinal Basil Hume remarked that

> It is within the space of fraternal life in common that each member's experience of God is allowed to mature. Within this space mutual love grows and is put into action; within this space freedom and solidarity no longer seem to be in conflict. One implies the other insofar as our lives are immersed in the paschal mystery.[4]

The magisterium of the community, as we can see, is profoundly linked to the ecclesiology of communion outlined by *Lumen gentium*. Its teaching aims to integrate each member of the monastic family into the Body of Christ, following the criteria laid down by John Paul II in *Tertio millennio adveniente* (n. 36) in a passage that asks for an examination of conscience as to the implementation of the Council's ecclesiology:

In the universal Church and in the particular Churches, is the ecclesiology of communion described in *Lumen Gentium* being strengthened? Does it leave room for charisms, ministries, and different forms of participation by the People of God, without adopting notions borrowed from democracy and sociology which do not reflect the Catholic vision of the Church and the authentic spirit of Vatican II?

What, then, defines the magisterium of the community? According to the vision passed on to us, we may say that it rests on the following factors:

- The perception of *my* community as the place of *my* conversion and *my* sanctification. There is no point in looking elsewhere for the tools I need to realize my vocation. No growth will spring from perilous wanderings in search of some kind of compensation. I am fully alive insofar as I cling to the reality into which Providence has seen fit to put me, that is, to my community, to my sisters, to my home. Insofar as I learn to belong in this reality, I grow toward an opening horizon. I am positively enabled to receive every gift of life.

- The recognition that the authority of my community, vested in individuals, is a blessed channel by which the Spirit speaks both to me as an individual and to the Church that surrounds me. Other words are efficacious insofar as they affirm my faithfulness to the authoritative word that is the touchstone of my life, to the word, that is, of my abbot or abbess.

- An endeavor to live out my relationships with my sisters as a constant search for life-giving communion, a search that requires me to be truly myself while fostering a truthful sense of belonging to my community. These relationships are built on affection. They make me capable of appreciating and nurturing the contribution of each one to my own good and the good of the house. They help me to grow in fidelity, mutual trust, and shared hope. They create an atmosphere that is genuinely humane. This is where the issue of fraternal and generational integration is lodged. Do we passionately desire to grow together as the Body of Christ? The building of relationships in community requires cordial cooperation, a readiness to speak with one another, a deliberate sharing of responsibility.

- A willingness to assume the tradition of the Order and my community as a seedbed of gratitude sprouting with life and grace, rendered fruitful by past history and future prospects.

- The resolve to move according to the particular grace of *my* community, which, for being an expression of the single Cistercian charism, has its own characteristics, its own story, its own development, its own vision, all reflecting the work of the Holy Spirit within it.

The long road toward integration and belonging starts in the novitiate. It sets out from that profound knowledge and acceptance of self that alone makes it possible to accept others, to be open to correction, to be passionate about conversion, to respond faithfully to authority, and to love the house. It continues through the monasticate, whose specificity resides in a more deliberate, in certain respects more crucifying, integration than that pursued in the novitiate, being more fully oriented toward becoming part of the adult community. We keep the experience alive in generational groups that meet to review life in common, when the sisters offer one another support and correction as they continue to sustain the formative grace of integration they received in their early years in the monastery. This effort to teach and learn results in a constant flow of understanding and gentleness from the older sisters toward the younger and back again. It facilitates the development of a common language, a common vision, and a shared tending toward *unanimitas*. *Unanimitas*, "oneness of mind and heart," was the Spirit's gift to the early Church, a gift ardently desired by the founders of Cîteaux. In a wonderful conference on the "common vision," given at Vitorchiano in 1994, Father Gregorio Penco told our community that

> For a correct appraisal of terminology (and not only of terminology), we must recall the importance attributed by monastic tradition to *unanimitas* as an expression of the *cor unum et anima una* that characterized the first Christian community (*cf.* Acts 4:32). This ideal has never ceased to shine brilliantly over the horizon of religious life in common. [. . .] It establishes a close relationship between the monastic community and the first Christian community.[5]

Were I to sum up the deepest tendency of our community's magisterium in a single word, I would say that it is exactly this: the search for *unanimitas*. Evidently, we never attain it fully. But we always desire it passionately.

The Synod on Consecrated Life recalled that fraternal life in common is a means by which the Church becomes a believable sign to the world, a clear historical model of that new way of living which Christ came to inaugurate on earth, expressed in solidarity and brotherhood with all human beings. What struck the inhabitants of Jerusalem to the quick when they contemplated the apostolic community was "how they loved one another" (*cf.* Acts 2:47; 4:33).[6] Of this there can be no doubt. To maintain this reality alive is surely the most convincing testimony we can bear to the vitality and boundless scope of the Christian proclamation.

The Path of Conversion

The fundamental points of reference for our pedagogy of conversion are the teaching of Scripture, the Rule of Saint Benedict (which puts the Gospel into practice for monks), and the spiritual doctrine of our Cistercian tradition. From the teaching of Scripture, we draw a notion that is especially crucial to our pedagogy. I refer to the notion of the *heart*, what we might call our "affective dimension," seen to constitute the core of human conversion and transformation:

> I will give them a new heart, and put a new spirit within them; I will remove the heart of stone from their flesh and give them a heart of flesh. (Ezek 11:19)

> A new heart I will give you, and a new spirit I will put within you; and I will remove from your body the heart of stone and give you a heart of flesh. (Ezek 36:26)

> He looked around at them with anger; he was grieved at their hardness of heart and said to the man, "Stretch out your hand." He stretched it out, and his hand was restored. (Mark 3:5)

How often have we not heard our novice mistresses say: "That girl has understood it all with her head, but her heart has not yet stirred!"

It goes without saying that our pedagogy presupposes a constant overlapping of the Bible, the Rule, and the Cistercian tradition. Insofar as a person is transformed by converging on God (*conversio ad*), he grows in obedience to the objective of the Rule, which works his inward unification. He learns to adhere to a specific spiritual heritage. It generates a new way of being human, in fidelity to the vocation by which we have been called.

To these fundamental principles of pedagogy, we must, of course, add an attentive listening to the nature and requirements of today's youth. What do they need in order to launch themselves on the path of transformation? We seek to appreciate their specific contribution, their particular way of being receptive to the monastic purpose and way of life. The challenge of transmission has always engaged us. We have thought about it carefully. We have been enriched through an attitude of listening, and this listening defines our way of encountering the young of today. I think we may say that the encounter has been fruitful. Our community endeavors to learn from everything and from everyone. It is disposed to being questioned by everything and everyone. It is aware of its poverty—also before the postulant who turned up yesterday. It is open to the newness of the Spirit, discernible even in the presumptuous young woman who is certain of knowing it all. During the course of our history, we have never ceased to have a real capacity for amazement and wonder before the gift of God, which embraces every creature with mercy. Our community remains sensitive to the signs that address our hearts *today*. But let us now pause briefly to consider two specific aspects of transmission.

The Teaching of the Rule

When Saint Gregory the Great tries to define the contemplative experience of Saint Benedict, he speaks of it as a *habitare secum*, "abiding or living with oneself." This *habitare secum* points to an interior, deep space in which we are truly our own and make our own choices. According to von Balthasar, the freedom of self-possession "is by no means alienated but rather inwardly fulfilled by consenting to that Being-in-its-totality which has now unveiled itself as that which freely

grounds all things, as that which, in infinite freedom, creates finite freedom."[1] At a symposium commemorating the
fifteenth centenary of the birth of Saint Benedict in 1980, the
French Dominican J. M. R. Tillard described the nature of a
Benedictine monastery as providing "spiritual space" in and
for the Church. Here is a generous passage from this important and masterful paper:

> In the third chapter of his [second] *Dialogue*, Gregory the
> Great explains to us the nature of the interior space we are
> talking about when he says that Saint Benedict, after the
> failure at Vicovaro, "lived with himself." He then goes on
> to answer the Deacon Peter's question about the mean-
> ing of "living with oneself." We find ourselves, here, at the
> heart of Tradition. Is it merely an indispensable minimum
> of interiority that is referred to? Gregory seems to be more
> categorical: "He went back to the wilderness he loved, to
> live alone with himself in the presence of his heavenly
> Father. [. . .] Blessed Benedict can be said to have 'lived
> with himself' because at all times he kept such close watch
> over his life and actions. By searching continually into his ·
> own soul he always beheld himself in the presence of his
> Creator. And this kept his mind from straying off to the
> world outside. [. . .] Now, the saintly Benedict really 'lived
> with himself' out in that lonely wilderness by always keep-
> ing his thoughts recollected." As he returned to his solitude,
> his holiness began to bud. Whereas the prodigal son "sank
> below himself," Benedict "left his own self far below" only
> when "drawn heavenward in fervent contemplation." The
> description reads awkwardly, but as soon as we interpret
> it in the light of Tradition, it becomes most suggestive. It
> gives us a key. Indeed, to say that someone "lives with him-
> self" is more or less to say that he remains in his quality of
> being made in the image and likeness of God. [. . .] Were
> we to employ the language of Pascal, we should say that
> it is fundamentally a matter of refusing "diversion," that
> is, the temptation of "the world" by which man is expelled
> from himself and lost in exterior agitation, drunk with the
> tumult that surrounds him, distracted from what should

be his principal concern. Emmanuel Mounier explains the term "diversion" in Pascal's terminology as "the immediate life deprived of memory, design, and control (which is the very definition of exteriority), unraveling within the human register of vulgarity." He goes on to give voice to the spirit of the Benedictine Rule when he affirms that "*personal* life begins when we are able to break with our environment, when we rein ourselves in and seize hold of ourselves with a view to gathering in a center, to becoming one." For the Rule proposes to lead the monk back to the center of himself and to keep him there. And this center is nothing other than the presence of the Lord in a human life.[2]

Any Benedictine pedagogy will as a matter of course focus on the first step of humility: the return to the heart. Intended by this phrase is the acquisition of humble self-knowledge. It tells us that the human conscience is able to live and learn the truth about itself in the presence of God. In his presence we come to possess ourselves in truth by accessing our ontological core: our original likeness to the Creator. Here, we may hope to seize the world, as Saint Benedict did, in an intuitive vision and see all creation gathered in a ball of light held by God's hand.

To Saint Bernard, this vital point represented the seal of divine likeness in our human nature. Eight centuries later, Thomas Merton referred to a luminous point at the heart of every person as the focal point of divine likeness and of what it is to be human. A related insight can be found in Franz Kafka, who intuited the presence in every creature of a point of ontological gravity, by which the creature is oriented toward the most radical meaning of its existence. This point of gravity seems to be the memory of a promised land stealing into the remembrance of individuals.

In a study conducted for the Regional Conference of the United States in 1992, Dom Bernard McVeigh of Our Lady of Guadalupe Abbey spoke of three features that he thought characteristic of the youth of that time, whom he found to be fundamentally rootless. He summarized these features as *self-absorption*, *anti-authoritarianism*, and *restlessness*. The experience, he says, of living in fatherless families, on the one hand, nurtures an angry, ironic perspective on parental figures and a rejection of authority; on the other hand, it stimulates a hunger for fatherhood and motherhood, sprung from lack of self-confidence, insecurity, and indecision. Paradoxically, these tendencies are accompanied by a strong need for self-affirmation that springs, precisely, from the absence of a father figure. A kind of self-absorption results, as each individual constructs a world of his or her own, a place of refuge where it is possible to be cut off from everything and everyone. There is no realism in such a world, and next to no ability to embrace reality as the arena of my own life and destiny. Instead I seek selfishly to evade the constraints of concrete living. I pursue personal gratification. I readily give myself up to a paralyzing, arid analysis of everything I am convinced I need but have not received. I make a stir in order to obtain what I deem to be indispensable for *my* life, clinging to every chance of obtaining what I want (though it immediately lets me down). And so the manifold malaise of our time is born: depression, instability, and victimization; a refusal to risk and dare; a horror of pain and sacrifice. In no way is this malaise confined to the young. Indeed, the human drama is fundamentally about the experience of feeling limited and finite. It produces an anguish that we do everything to forget, in a flight from ourselves and from reality that often finds expression in bids for power, in competitiveness, and in violence.

In his Apostolic Letter *Tertio millennio adveniente*, Pope John Paul II identified the sins that most gravely threaten the unity of humankind: irresponsibility, a want of discernment, and a crisis of doubt. The latter he saw to be linked with a crisis of obedience with regard to the Church's Magisterium (nn. 35–36). These destructive forces corrode the cohesion of Church and secular society alike. They engender deep-seated divisions and intolerance.

In its insistence on the "return to the heart," the Rule of Saint Benedict provides a most potent tool for teaching a person how to enter into the process of conversion. We return to the heart not only by interiorizing the defining values of our vocation or the necessary, irreplaceable structures that make those values manifest. Much more important, we return to the heart if we recover our own interiority, if we attain to the core of our own being, the vital point of divine likeness that lies deep within us. The God who is Love makes himself and his redemption known in this inward space where we encounter ourselves in the light of his Word. Rooted anew at the heart of our God-given being, we are enabled little by little to face the truth about ourselves without fear. We discover ourselves to be known and redeemed by the God who is Love. On this basis we gain the maturity we need to confront our fears, emotions, and revolts, the fragility of our affective life and our disordered inclinations. Saint Bernard speaks of discovering the "sewers of memory." The light of the Word of God, filtered by our superiors and by the Church, helps us to be reconciled with ourselves, with the truth of our misery and grandeur, with our limitations and our infinite destiny. In the process, we learn to call everything that stirs within us by its right name. This is the holy realism of the Rule. It does battle against everything that is approximate, relative, and superficial. It does battle, too, against every form of flight from reality. It causes our sublimations, the charade of our myriad excuses, and the vague rationalization that compromise human freedom and truth to fade.

Obsculta, o fili: "Listen, my son," are the initial words of the Prologue to the Rule of Saint Benedict. We return to our heart above all by listening. Our progress toward interior listening is aided immeasurably by *lectio divina*, the deep, continuous rumination of the Word of God by which the Word takes root within us and becomes an essential criterion of discernment and judgment, shaping us into the *forma Christi* by which we long to be defined. We live in a frantic, noisy world that not only hinders our ability to listen but threatens to paralyze it. Often, we hear only ourselves spouting the self-approbation dictated by current fashion. Conversion and change, transformation and transfiguration, meanwhile, happen through a profound owning of truth that can only take place in silence. It is in silence that the Word becomes Presence. In this silence we also become more open to the objective words that address us through our superior's teaching, through the impact of correction, or through the purification wrought by the common life. There is such a thing as spiritual deafness. It stands for a refusal to depend on others. It stands for apathy and distancing with regard to interior change. It is interesting to note how Father Benedetto Calati associates Benedict's *habitare secum* with the faculty of vision, where vision is understood as openness to seize the presence of God in the present moment, pregnant with eternity, and to perceive present reality as the initial manifestation of the Kingdom of God.[3] This relation between vision and presence permits the growth of a common outlook. This in turn fosters a community's *unanimitas*.

Throughout the Rule we encounter an extraordinary regard for concrete, real, and present things. Saint Benedict is forever concerned with gestures. He wants norms to be realized in concrete acts and so invests the present moment with enormous significance: "Such as these, therefore, immediately leaving their own affairs and forsaking their own will, dropping the work they were engaged in and leaving it unfinished, with the ready step of obedience follow up with their deeds the voice of him who commands" (RB 5.8). It is the here-and-now that counts. That is why we think there are no surer criteria for discerning a vocation than a person's response to the actual reality of common life, his readiness to fit in and to be of service. The qualities we look for in discernment, in fact, tend to be articulated in terms such as these: an ability to change; an ability to belong; an ability to embrace real life; an ability to assume responsibility for the vocation received so as to motivate it; an ability to see oneself as unfinished, in process of transformation and with constant need for conversion. Above all, our monastic pedagogy emphasizes self-knowledge and a clear understanding of our vocation before the face of God. Hence, it also stresses our responsibility with regard to ourselves and with regard to our community in a never-ending process of dynamic conversion. The Rule provides countless elements toward a monastic pedagogy. If we have here only mentioned a few, it is because these have in a special way shaped our experience, our community's way of thinking about discernment.

The Teaching of Our Fathers

It is quite clear that, for Saint Bernard, the process of conversion is enacted essentially through the return from the region of unlikeness to the region of likeness. These terms, drawn from the parable of the Prodigal Son, indicate a passage that takes place on several levels:

- from what is my own to what is held in common;
- from caprice to true freedom;
- from self-will to good will;
- from sewage-memory to mercy-memory;
- from carnal affection to spiritual love;
- from rebellious disobedience to filial obedience.

We are here dealing with a far-reaching, well-configured process of conversion that in the last instance develops Saint Benedict's *habitare secum*, even as it spells out the "return to the heart" that is the essence of the Rule and that, for Saint Bernard, is no less the essence of conversion. When expounding this theme, I always like to quote from one of Saint Bernard's most pleasant and most profound treatises, his *Life of Saint Malachy*. In this work, Bernard tells of an ecclesiastic who maintained, in the face of magisterial teaching, that error had crept into the Church's doctrine about the Eucharist. Malachy put the man right and invited him to recant, but the ecclesiastic's pride would not compromise: "I will not forsake the truth for the sake of being a respecter of persons," he said. It was a matter of *his* truth, of course, and the saintly bishop replied as follows: "May God make you confess the truth, by constraint, if need be." Bernard tells us that the ecclesiastic, on his way home, suddenly took ill and fell on the ground by the road. And then follows the passage that concerns us here:

> A vagabond who was out of his mind happened to arrive at the place and asked the man why he was lingering there. [The ecclesiastic] answered that he was in the grip of grave illness and unfit either to proceed or to go back. The madman said: "This illness is nothing other than very death!" He did not say this of himself, but God fittingly used a madman to rebuke one who had refused to comply with the sane counsels of sensible men. And he added: "*Revertere domum*. Go home! I shall help you."[4]

Revertere domum carries exactly the same sense as *redire ad cor*: go back to the place of your conversion; go back to that space of interiority and humility, listening and obedience. There you will be delivered from the infirmity that confines you to the dust of pride. *Revertere domum!* The cry, for Bernard, is a passionate one. It calls us to abandon a life that, for being brilliantly reasonable, is merely directed outward, to return to a life centered on humble listening to the truth. This listening effects the freeing of the heart. It acknowledges the limitations of human reason and shows how these can be overcome through a clinging to faith. Through obedience, the heart becomes sensitive to the boundless truth of the spirit. It translates what it hears into concrete acts. Thus man is led back to his core, his *domus*, to the *home* of his own heart.

Bernard characteristically pursues two lines of thought at the same time. The first concerns self-knowledge and falls under anthropology. The second concerns configuration to Christ and falls under theology. On the level of anthropology Bernard really surpasses modern approaches of psychoanalysis inasmuch as he never bases himself solely on analytical inquiry into personality conflicts (though such analysis is never absent from his introspection). Going beyond pure analysis, Bernard's approach is fundamentally concerned with the call of God. In the last instance, it is this call, rather than auto-analysis, that dramatically confronts man with himself, with his own truth and responsibility. In this optic, the measure of man is not his inner conflicts but the response he owes to life and to the author of life. Bernard is emphatic that the first degree of truth into which we enter involves self-knowledge *in the light of the Word of God*, a knowledge that is never content with the *status quo*: it always spurs us on toward a response, toward recognition of personal responsibility before God. For what is the effect of illumination by the Word, asks Saint Bernard, if not self-knowledge?

> It opens the book of the conscience, passes in review the wretched sequence of life, unfolds the sad events of its history, enlightens the reason and, the memory having leafed, as it were, it is set before its own eyes. What is more, these two [memory and reason] are not so much faculties of the soul as the soul itself, so that it is both observer and observed: it appears resolved against itself and is dragged by these heavy-handed officers before its own assizes to be judged by its own thoughts.[5]

Saint Bernard gives prominence to the faculties of memory and will when he describes the way that leads toward self-knowledge. He conceives of the human soul as a composite of reason, memory, and will. It is as a result of sin, he says, that our reason has lost its sight, our memory its shape, and our will the freedom to move. He dramatically evokes the war waged by memory and will against reason in order to justify further the behavior of carnal man:

Do not hope to hear from me what it is within your memory that your reason detects, censures, judges, and sentences. Apply your hearing within, roll back the eyes of your heart, and you will learn by your own experience what is going on. [. . .] Even though all the itching of evil pleasure quickly passes and any charm of sensual satisfaction is short-lived, still it stamps on the memory certain bitter marks; it leaves filthy traces. Into that reservoir, as into a sewer, all these disgusting and dirty thoughts drizzle and run off. Weighty is the book wherein have been inscribed all these acts with the pen of truth.[6]

When a man sets out on the path of conversion, however, the role of memory takes on a positive aspect. Reason awakens and takes account of its misery. It sees its misery and recognizes the filth that is invading memory. Thus, from the awareness of such a serious predicament, it learns to beg for help. At that point, memory is no longer a stinking sewer of lies. It is transformed instead into a remembrance of mercy received:

This also is a counsel of devotion, that the man who is displeasing to himself is pleasing to God, and he who hates his own house, that is to say a house full of filth and wretchedness, is invited to the house of glory, a house not made with hands, eternal in the heavens. It is no wonder if he trembles with awe at the greatness of this honor and finds it hard to believe what he has heard, if he starts in astonishment and says, "Is it possible for such wretchedness to make a man happy?" Whoever you are, if you are in this frame of mind, do not despair: it is mercy, not misery, that makes a man happy, but mercy's natural home is misery. Indeed it happens that misery becomes the source of man's happiness when humiliation turns into humility and necessity becomes a virtue.[7]

The humble heart remembers everything it has received from God's mercy. It becomes merciful to the extent that it recalls the mercy bestowed on itself. So often, our praying of the Psalms invites us to remember good things received. The remembrance of mercy is the savor of truth in every circumstance. It signals the perception that God's mercy is present in every time and space of the human condition. Only through intense personal experience of this fact will we be led to pass from an arrogance that is easily scandalized, that sits in judgment on others, to a merciful compassion and openness to others. This is when our life becomes *contemplative*, a space charged with God's living Presence, a manifestation of saving Mercy.

Our will, memory's companion, is given us as a pledge of the freedom we possess as sons of God. We all know that famous passage from the treatise on *Grace and Free Will* in which Bernard distinguishes between good will (which is dependence of God) and evil will (which is non-dependence):

> Created, then, to a certain extent, as our own in freedom of will, we become God's as it were by good will. Moreover, he makes the will good, who made it free; and makes it good to this end, that we may be a kind of firstfruits of his creatures; because it would have been better for us never to have existed than that we should remain always our own. For those who wished to belong to themselves, became indeed like gods, knowing good and evil; but then they were not merely their own, but the devil's. Hence, free will makes us our own; bad will, the devil's; and good will, God's.[8]

Bernard stresses the threefold blessing the will incurs, first from *creation* (since God created it good), next from *freedom* (which shows that we are made in the image of God), finally from *conversion* (which involves the deliberate, loving submission of our will to God). This submission is what Bernard calls "justice." Christ himself proclaims it blessed: "Blessed are those who hunger and thirst for justice, for they shall be satisfied" (Matt 5:6). Saint Paul likewise lauds it in his Letter to the Romans: "But thanks be to God that you, having once been slaves of sin, have become obedient from the heart to the form of teaching to which you were entrusted" (6:17).

At last, Bernard turns his attention to reason. He considers it in close connection with a faith-enlightened conscience and so defines it as the ability to discern and make judgments in the light of the Word of God. Thus he reminds us that the fullest expression of human reason resides not in critical or logical skill but in faith. The act of faith, for Bernard, does not belong to the sphere of pure speculation, nor is it a rationalizing act. It is, rather, unitive. By it, we entrust ourselves to Another and cling to him. We decide to follow a *Person*, that is, Christ.

By way of summary, and in order to encapsulate the pedagogy of conversion we have developed at Vitorchiano, it may be useful to list the principal stages of the process:

- A recovery of interior unity as we own the truth about ourselves before God.

- A return to the core of our own being, to our heart, in order there to let ourselves be judged by the Word of God, of the Church, and of our superiors so that this Word may reveal the truth about our destiny and shape our existence.

- A right deployment of memory in order to acknowledge and take on board our own past, assuming it as an experience of mercy and so being made open to receive the gift of compassion.

- An engagement of the will to hand ourselves over to God as his *property*, rejecting the autonomy that springs from rebellion.

These stages must be constantly realized in the dense reality of today, in concrete daily living. We must refuse to seek refuge in abstraction, rationalization, and daydreaming.

Conversion and Affectivity

At the outset we spoke of the teaching of the Scriptures. We cited the Prophet Ezekiel's striking insistence on the heart of flesh: "I will give them a new heart, and put a new spirit within them; I will remove the heart of stone from their flesh and give them a heart of flesh" (Ezek 11:19). An authentic process of conversion touches, or rather seizes, every aspect of our being. It transforms our way of thinking and alters our behavior. It even affects our bodies. The clearest sign of genuine conversion, however, is the transformation of a "heart of stone" into a "heart of flesh." It is God, evidently, who works this transformation, but our human freedom must choose whether or not it will set out toward conversion, whether it wishes to *return*.

I do not intend, here, to enter into the problems connected with the development and maturing of our affective nature. We shall deal with them later on. For the present I simply want to stress that the affective dimension is of paramount importance in a person's conversion to God. In working out our pedagogy of formation, we have learned, through pain and disappointment, that the concern with a merely outward perfection of observance in fact constitutes an all but insuperable obstacle to a person's growth in conversion. The security, even pride, that is generated by monastic perfectionism never issues in the warmth of genuine affection, compassion, pardon, tenderness, and maternity. The conversion of any human being presupposes the dissolution of a certain rigidity of reason, hardness of heart, and violence of criticism. At the heart of our obstinacy, there is always a stone that must be shattered and give way to flesh. But what precisely is the heart of flesh that comes alive through conversion? To illustrate what it consists in, we might quote the exhortation with which the community of Vitorchiano addressed the sisters of one of its foundations when, in 1991, they changed their canonical stability from the motherhouse to their new community:

> So far, your chief concern has perhaps been the establishment of a robust level of observance and a dedication to work. At this point, though, it is necessary to make space

in your hearts for the growth of freer, more cordial relationships among the sisters. There is a need to make space for
greater human warmth, for a genuine tenderness that is full
of respect for the other. By this we do not intend compli-
ments and flattery, which are of no use whatever. We intend
a smiling openness to the other, an openness that widens the
heart. You must become more human, more cordial. By your
affection for one another you will grow as persons and build
up your community. The vow of stability you are about to
make is about precisely this. It involves the risk to love more
and listen better, to be more understanding and trustful.

We find this outlook confirmed in a remark made by Saint
Rafael Arnáiz Barón, our brother from the monastery of San
Isidro de Dueñas who died in 1938, at age twenty-seven:

> When before I looked for a religious and instead found a
> run-of-the-mill man . . . how I suffered. Good God! [. . .]
> In the midst of all that (I see it clearly now), there was plenty
> of pride, much vanity and immense self-love. [. . .] Now a
> very unusual thing is happening to me. Some days, when I
> come from prayer, although it seems to me that I am doing
> nothing, I feel very strong desires, I yearn with a great long-
> ing to love all the members of the community as Jesus loves
> them. [. . .] Just as before I would become very disturbed
> upon seeing a failure or a weakness in a brother and would
> almost feel revulsion, now I feel a very great tenderness
> toward him and would like to make reparation for the fault
> insofar as I can.[9]

Now this is a sign of authentic charity. Rafael is no longer
scandalized by the limitations of others. He ceases to criticize
the weaknesses he observes and instead enters into an experience of true compassion, understanding, and tenderness. He
receives this new, positive attitude toward the brethren as a
precious gift from the Lord, convinced as he is that nothing
good can come out of himself. The love welling up in his heart
is, he says, a stupendous miracle wrought in him by the Spirit:
the gift of a heart of flesh. The heart of flesh, then, is the seal

of conversion. By it, Rafael's countenance has been formed into the humble, gentle face of Christ.

The Cistercian tradition, in fact, unanimously affirms that it is fundamental to let our affectivity be converted. Certainly, it is by virtue of our reason that we first realize what is good and where the good can be found. But until our affective nature too is turned toward the good, our will remains unchanged, and reason itself has a hard time of it. Saint Bernard sagely describes the dynamics involved in his treatise *De conversione*. From the very beginning, the monastic tradition has insisted on contrition and weeping. This confirms what we have been saying: *sentiment* too, our affective powers, must be engaged in the process that was initiated by lucid rationality. Otherwise the progress toward love remains fruitless. It will never issue in tears of pardon and the engagement of compassion.

Our monastic pedagogy hinges on the necessity of passing, through conversion, from the heart of stone to the heart of flesh. This passage constitutes an ever-present criterion in our work of formation. It involves a battle against every form of aggression, intolerance, and discrimination revealed by our common life. We are all conditioned by our instincts and by a certain intrinsic violence. For that reason, it is no easy matter to make space for gentleness, patience, and kindness. What matters most is to have a clear sense of who we are and to make a concerted effort to transform our stony heart into living flesh.

I should like to conclude this section with a passage from Jan Dobraczynski's book *Encounters with the Black Madonna*. It cites a conversation Cardinal Wyszynski once had with Pope John XXIII while the two of them were strolling in the Vatican Gardens. "My dear son," said the pope,

> people aren't bad. What happens is that they do not know how to love. How, then, can we teach them to love? Only by loving. That is why the Lord gives us a family when we come into the world. A loving family engenders loving

persons. I am sure you know this very well. When I came
to pray at Częstochowa (how I struggle to pronounce that
name!), it struck me very much that she, Our Lady, desires more than anything else to be our mother. My dear, I
think we must follow her example and love everyone with
a mother's love. If we did, then slowly, slowly, we would
gain the whole world.[10]

A loving community engenders loving persons. In our community, we have had that experience. This simple insight
provides, I think, the best possible conclusion to our brief reflection on the engagement of the heart in Christian formation.
If the heart remains unengaged, how can a person possibly
attain to life-giving maturity?

On Teaching How to Love

When our community meets to discern the progress of one of our candidates for profession, certain themes often recur. The most important of these can be summarized in the following observations, pregnant with aspirations that concern us all:

- As we move ahead on the path of love, we must exorcise the fears that beset our affective lives.

- We should not fear difficulties. *Everything* can help us grow as long as we do not enclose ourselves in possessive self-absorption.

- It is not love that presents difficulties. Love develops the entire affective potential of a person. What creates problems is not loving *enough*. By not loving enough we remain standing on the threshold of affective risk without ever opening the door into a giving and receiving that is radically free. We are frightened by the fragility of our capacity for love, by the selfishness that distorts it and by the sublimations that render love unreal. So often a spotless surface covers an impure harshness further down.

- We want people who are prepared to risk explicit tenderness and who are capable of admiring others in a pure way. We want them to run the risk of uncalculating trust, to find joy in the common life without shying away from the work required to become one with the community, to embrace this work, rather, as a way of opening wide the heart. Then we shall have more frequent occasion to taste "how good and how pleasant it is when brothers live in unity!" (Ps 133:1). We want people who recognize that they can only love if they accept to be hurt, that only if we die to ourselves does our love become stronger than death. We want them to see that, if they find little love in or around themselves, the deficit probably springs from a fear of being hurt.

Let us try, then, to articulate these insights, so important to our monastic pedagogy, in a clearer, more coherent and synthetic manner while remaining conscious that what we have to say will of necessity be fragmentary—and probably very subjective too.

The Problem of Today

Until not so long ago in our part of the world, the commonly accepted measure of affective maturity was a person's ability to control his or her emotions. Building on a Stoic model, it looked out for reason's mastery of sentiment. Any behavior motivated by the bodily, emotional, passionate, even sensible sphere was considered more or less sinful. With the passage of time, however, something exploded. Indeed, the natural rhythm of time has been upset by a series of loud, garish factors. Life now is moving at an increasingly fast speed. As a result, our outlook on the world, on time and space, is no longer what it was. We are conditioned by simultaneity. It makes us able to gather masses of information in the twinkle of an eye, though we are less able to invest this information with the density of patient reflection. As a result, our behavior has changed. Our ability to assimilate is subject to overload, producing a sense of indigestion, so well described by Jean-Paul Sartre in his *Nausea*. What is at the heart of this drama? It is the fear of having to face up to our intrinsic freedom in a setting of universal relativism, a setting that renders freedom irrelevant. Alternatively, it amounts to a dark fear of solitude in an existential vortex, void of lasting sense.

We find this fear poignantly voiced by Françoise Sagan. In *Aimez-vous Brahms?*, Simon says to Paule: "You should be condemned to death, you should be condemned to solitude! I can imagine nothing worse, nothing more inevitable. It frightens me more than anything, and everyone else, too. Still no one admits it. I am frightened. I am frightened."[1] Françoise Sagan lived in a world without ideals. When she was young, one model seemed as good as another, and so she never passed beyond the *Carpe diem* of happy memory, giving it expression in the illusory, precarious nature of love that leads by default to despair: "One day you will cease to love me, and one day, no doubt, I will also cease to love you, and we shall be alone again. And another year will have passed."[2]

At stake, as Charles Moeller comments, is a fear of everyday life, "when we stand in the rain waiting for the nine-o'clock bus."[3] "One day there will be nothing left, just darkness, absence, death." "To be but a provisional breath on a millionth part of one of a billion galaxies."[4] Here we see it again, that anguish in the face of existence, provoked by the impact of loneliness or exposure, by a sense of fragmentation brought on by sensual pleasure or by sheer nothingness. The anguish takes shape against the backdrop of loneliness. It is, to cite Moeller again, a "spontaneous anxiety [. . .] that imperceptibly colors the whole of life without our being aware of it, apart from deliberate acts of will."[5] It is a kind of disenchanted, rather cynical wisdom in whose perspective life seems altogether ephemeral, brief, and pointless.

The heroes of Sagan's books are normally orphans. They are reluctant to leave a particular kind of infancy. They are frightened of life and of the responsibilities life confers. Without having truly emerged from their mothers' wombs, they constantly seek to return to the womb in order to be protected and enveloped. They create moments of gratification for themselves through fugitive, tragically occasional instances of sexual or emotional intimacy. They escape into the worlds of drugs or violence, or into a vague perception of reality beyond this earth through dabbling in the occult, in sects, or in Eastern spirituality, as often happens nowadays too.

In Sagan's novels we seem to be light-years away from the thought world of another young, brilliantly talented writer who was only twenty years older than Sagan: Etty Hillesum. Etty was twenty-nine years old in 1943 when she perished in Auschwitz, having passed from the most arid kind of atheism to a passionate encounter with God *through pain*. These few brief passages provide us with windows into her soul:

> Even if one's body aches, the spirit can continue to do its work, can it not? It can love and *hineinhorchen*—"hearken into"—itself and unto others and unto what binds us to life. *Hineinhorchen*—I so wish I could find a Dutch equivalent for that German word. Truly, my life is one long hearkening unto my self and unto others, unto God. And if I say that I hearken, it is really God who hearkens inside me.[6]

> With the passing of people, I feel a growing need to speak to You alone. I love people so terribly because in every human being I love something of You.[7]

> I have broken my body like bread and shared it out among men.[8]

> We should be willing to act as a balm for all wounds.[9]

> It is the only thing we can do. [. . .] I see no alternative, each of us ought to destroy in himself all that he thinks he ought to destroy in others.[10]

> If I should survive and keep saying, "Life is beautiful and meaningful," they will have to believe me.[11]

> For once you have begun to walk with God, you need only keep on walking with Him and all of life becomes one long stroll—such a marvellous feeling.[12]

> There will always be a small patch of sky above, and there will always be enough space to fold two hands in prayer.[13]

But the shipwreck of World War II is lodged in the past and has, alas, been all but forgotten. A new society has been formed, devoted to wellbeing and consumerism. Ideals that, in the postwar years, made themselves intensively felt have atrophied in a calculated grasping at the here-and-now. Our fixation on sex often masks a deadening of feeling that is ever more in evidence. Theoretical analysis seems set to justify the conflicts wrought by our selfishness and cowardice. A new kind of cannibalism has entered our attitudes to abortion, euthanasia, extremist nationalism, and ethnic intolerance. Human beings are readily sacrificed in the interest of efficiency. The youth of today have grown up in a world conditioned by such malaise. And they are the ones we must teach how to love.

By all means, a person who has encountered Jesus Christ *has* encountered love, and love everlasting. Among the young people of today there are some, thank God, who in their families, in the Church, or in Christian movements have had very healthy experiences of friendship, encounter, and true humanity. It is young people of this kind who normally (but not always) are drawn to monastic life. I am convinced, however, that the very consciousness of today's youth has been decisively formed, or *de*formed, by a certain kind of literature, a certain kind of existential vision, that presents life as ultimately void of sense. And who is to say if the relativist, consumerist mentality of our time, the media's superficiality, the pop culture that conforms a young person's aspirations to the lowest common denominator, do not leave an impact every bit as strong as ideology?

The generation of 1968 had fought for emancipation and great ideals. It wanted to bring about a clean break with a corrupt and tired grown-up world by violently affirming the eternal dream of a purer world, of a free, loving, and unselfish humanity. The generations that have followed it have demythologized these ideals.

With the generation of 1968, one could still quarrel and fight in order to uphold some truth, to defend some value. It entertained ideals of hope. It carried utopia in its heart. It was passionate, enthusiastic, and rebellious. Today's youth are very different. They seek above all to maintain a certain facade. They want the tranquillity conferred by success (difficult to come by on the battlefield of market forces and youth unemployment), the reassurance of convenience. We note the growth of a particular kind of moral void that goes hand in hand with a thirst for meaning that is enacted in sometimes ambivalent efforts to find belonging, trust, and a sense of accomplishment in life.

The Teaching of the Magisterium

What does it mean to teach someone to love? More than anything else, it means *re*-educating in him or her the faculty of love. Such formation in love is at the heart of true chastity. We sometimes intuit this in a flash, although we often invest the *vow* of chastity with a sense that is very formal and rather negative. It may be that we have never been further removed from this true value of chastity than we are now. Yet (and this is a paradox) we have perhaps never been closer to a real understanding of what it means. We owe this understanding to Pope John Paul II's theology of the body, which has, in a way, laid the foundations for a new anthropology. We are well equipped, now, to approach Saint Bernard's "degrees of love" with fresh insight. On Maundy Thursday in 1981, the pope spoke as follows about love:

> The washing of the feet manifests a readiness to transform the world and to restore it to the Father. The world is transformed, really transformed, by love. About to pass from this world, Jesus gave his disciples this commandment: "I give you a new commandment: love one another as I have loved you" (John 13:34). The readiness to transform the world by love is manifest in the washing of the feet we are about to perform. [. . .] To wash someone's feet is to serve. Only the person who truly serves transforms the world in order to restore it to the Father.[14]

A few months later he added the following insight, in an address to married people: "We must constantly learn this kind of love. We must learn it patiently, on our knees."[15] So how do we learn to love? We learn it by praying, by serving, and by loving.

The teaching of John Paul II goes into much greater depth. Over and beyond what he expounded in his Wednesday Catechesis, he articulated it in a number of texts, especially in his book *Love and Responsibility*. In this book's chapters on the true meaning of chastity, Karol Wojtyła explains with clarity how we cannot possibly understand the meaning of chastity unless we first envisage love as a function of genuine reciprocity between persons, as a *communio personarum*, with particular stress on the principle of integration through service, through a solidarity we desire and ever choose anew.

Love does not fall under psychology. It belongs fully in the sphere of the moral life. Love, then, is a virtue. Only by being a virtue (having the moral weight and value required to mobilize our reason and will) does it correspond to the human person's need to love and be loved. Chastity is not reducible to repression or control of blind instinct. If it were, it would simply provide dynamite for uncontrollable explosions. Chastity is the freeing of love, man's affective potential, from the limitation and selfish possessiveness of sensuality, from self-centred sentimentality. Chastity renders our deepest interiority transparent. It sets our heart free to give and receive. It lets us love without counting costs or calculating profit.[16]

John Paul II places love at the heart of the religious vocation, which he understands as a way of committing oneself utterly for the sake of a clearly defined goal. A vocation constitutes an ideal that lays claim to every aspect of a person. As a human response to a divine call, a vocation necessarily involves not only love but the gift of self made for the sake of love. The pope observes that, "in the light of the Gospel, it is obvious that every man solves the problem of his vocation in practice above all by adopting a conscious personal attitude toward the supreme demand made on us in the commandment to love."[17]

Whatever a person's vocation might be, it is essential that love, as a measure of our affectivity and our potential for self-giving, should animate the response we give, through our vocation, to life as a whole. Otherwise we could hardly call it a "vocation" or a vital choice. We should be dealing with nothing but a fruitless erring to and fro in the closed world of instinct, with people passing through continuous changes without making any stable commitment, without running any risk, without ever letting the features of their countenance be fully defined.

The "theology of communion" that issued from the Second Vatican Council has increasingly been reminding us how crucial it is that love, the charity of Christ, should inform our human relationships to ennoble them with respect and understanding, to fill them with deliberate generosity in giving and receiving. The Synod on Consecrated Life reaffirmed such fraternal reciprocity as a criterion by which to evaluate the authenticity of a vocation. In the absence of an authentic fraternal life, religious life itself cannot be authentic.

I have noticed that certain authors daringly refer to the religious life as a "sacrament of friendship." It does appear as a visible sign of communion in this world of ours, which market forces would transform into a multitude of solitary and competitive people. Yes, it seems to be a "sacrament of friendship." Religious feel a genuine need for the living space provided by their life in common, for that is where they live and grow in their response to God's call. When they are away from it, they are homesick. It is for them a true school of charity. I remember our own Mother Sebastiana who, when away from the monastery, called Vitorchiano her "Jerusalem." Until the last breath of her short life, she longed to set eyes on it again. In her, Saint Bernard's oft-recorded homesickness for Clairvaux echoes for our own time.

The recent documents of the Magisterium call for no comment of mine. We simply need to be constantly rereading them to keep mining their rich significance.

The Church provides us with an orientation that is crystal clear. We are to educate people in such a way that they become capable of love, of faithful giving and receiving, of generosity in their striving to become part of the community, of a trust that knows how to affirm others. These are precisely the values Saint Benedict speaks about under the heading of "good zeal" (RB 72.1), which is his short-hand for generous, cordial service in obedience to the Lord's commandment. At stake is a Gospel imperative that no religious life in common can afford to neglect, least of all a monastery, haunted as it is by the ideal and example held out to us by the early Church, where all believers had but one heart and one soul (*cf.* Acts 5:32).

It certainly is not easy to teach others how to love today, for in the young we often find a self-satisfied attitude that seems to proclaim, "I couldn't care less!"—a tendency to criticize the community and individuals within it with a negativity whose real purpose is to attract attention. We are dealing with a possessive strategy of people placing themselves at the center of others' concern. Often we find them resorting to irony as a way of defending their own fear of love. We see that their understanding of the *communio personarum* is merely emotional. And they do not think twice about dumping all their own trials, frustrations, and arrogant judgment onto the community or society in which they live and which, naturally, "does not understand me." Even monks sometimes give in to a sense of being the *victim* of given situations, a temptation that ultimately signifies a refusal to assume the pain of conversion.

The texts of the Magisterium, meanwhile, leave no room for doubt. The document *The Fraternal Life in Common* does not shy away from affirming that it is only by loving that we build ourselves up. And only by building ourselves up in love do we build up the Church in communion. Only a person capable of love can enter the realm of trinitarian communion, the eucharistic dimension of human community. The malaise of our young people does reveal a desire for love. And if this desire expresses itself in contradictory ways, it is our responsibility to educate it.

The Teaching of the Cistercian Tradition

Our community first articulated its criteria for formation in this area based on the teaching of our Cistercian Fathers, which we rediscovered and learned to see in a new light thanks to the teaching of today's Church. It is impossible, within the bounds of this book, to attempt a synthesis of what these masters of the Cistercian school of charity taught: a special study would be called for. First of all, we should have to expound the Fathers' anthropology. Then it would be necessary to go through the itinerary for a growth in love set before us by Saint Bernard in his *Degrees of Love*, from the first, most carnal step (the love of ourselves for our own sake) through the following steps (in which we learn, first, to love the Other for our own sake, then to love him for what he is in himself) to a love that is fully pure and fully free, the love of ourselves for *God's* sake, a love we shall taste in fullness only when we reach paradise.

It is likewise obvious that we cannot here embark on an analysis with a view to identifying the potential of these teachings, in large measure still unexplored, or looking for possible links with the findings of modern psychoanalysis. Nor have we the time and space to explore how William of Saint-Thierry or Aelred of Rievaulx, not to mention Bernard himself, applied doctrine in concrete monastic instruction. I cannot, though, simply pass over this material in silence, and so I must content myself with a few brief indications by way of example. And here I must say that we find what is possibly the freest, richest, most exuberant (and so most fascinating) expression of Cistercian affectivity in that great thirteenth-century Benedictine, Saint Gertrude, who was a true daughter of Saint Bernard.

Saint Gertrude's spiritual experience moved in its totality around and within the Heart of Jesus. It expanded through the revelation of that Heart as a place of light, a dwelling of delight, an abode of indescribable joy. Saint Gertrude's language is passionate and free. She arrived, she says, at intimacy with the Heart of God after her major conversion, which she refers to as a "passing" from the world of speculative thought (for which her intelligence and culture singularly equipped her) to the world of gratuitous love in a faith that utterly abandons itself to mystery. It has sometimes been said of Saint Gertrude that she was self-absorbed. I would be more inclined to speak of the *intimate* character of her spirituality. She does not revel in emotional or psychological introspection but readily crosses the threshold of mystical intimacy with astonishing affective freedom.

Saint Gertrude's message must be clearly distinguished from the devotion to the Sacred Heart that found expression at Paray-Le-Monial four centuries later. To an age conditioned by the disincarnate tendency of Jansenism, the more modern devotion revealed the merciful humanity of the Heart of Christ. But Saint Gertrude's experience did not issue from a private devotion. It was an expression of the liturgical dimension of her monastic life and evolved at the heart of her community's shared choral prayer, in the prayerful spirit of her monastery. Her sisters described her as profoundly devout, humble, and magnanimous, and above all as a woman of great freedom. Gertrude is quintessentially free. Her freedom makes her an exceptional lover, so that the affective language of her writings seems positively frightening to us, impure and unfree as we are, prone to be scandalized by her enamored, crystalline excesses. Her vocabulary is Bernardine: *Liquefacit intima mea*, she says ("he melts my inner being"), and this state of liquefaction is quite habitual for her. She speaks of rivers arising out of the Lord's heart. She "licks" the wellspring of living water, "is immersed" in the torrent that overflows from it, "gets drunk" at the river-head.

Gertrude has a very strong experience of the Blood of Jesus purifying her, washing over her, and making her pass from a state of great aridity to an immersion in deep waters. This is where her transformation is effected. Little by little, she *becomes* liquid. Then, while she rests in Jesus' bosom, liquefaction gives way to vaporization. Her heart evaporates. It turns into a censer from which sweet smells rise.

At the heart of this incredible experience of overflowing love, Gertrude becomes conscious of her sinfulness, of the distraction of her heart that tries to pull her away from the intimacy to which the Lord draws her back constantly and mysteriously. She recalls an occasion on which worldly conversation had so distracted her that she had neglected the indwelling presence of the Lord for several days: "Your gentle humility, and the wonderful goodness of your wonderful divine love, saw me in such a state of abandoned madness that I did not care that I had lost such a treasure."[18] Gertrude's generous affectivity makes her reach out to serve others, while service leads her back to love:

> Then whenever it happens that I must devote myself to external works for practical purposes, may I be given to them on loan, as special cases: then when they have been perfectly completed to your praise, may I return at once to you in my heart of hearts, as the general rule, just as the tumultuous rush of water flows back to the depths, when whatever barred the way has been removed.[19]

The "depths," for Gertrude, always indicate the heart of Christ. Gertrude's final "passage" is the passage of divinization. To express it she, like Saint Bernard, has recourse to the affective image of the kiss:

> As for the gracious gift of your most pleasing kiss, sometimes when I sit concentrating on you in my innermost being, reading the Canonical Hours or Vigils for the dead, you often in the course of a single psalm plant a sweet kiss on my mouth ten times over or more. This kiss surpasses all aromatic fragrance and honeyed draught. I have also noticed your most loving gaze often directed at me, and sensed your close and firm embrace in my soul.[20]

It is from such passionate affectivity that Gertrude extends her vision to embrace the whole Church. In the epilogue to her second book of Revelations, she makes the following prayer for the present time of earthly pilgrimage during which believers look forward to seeing God's glory in heaven:

> But meantime, according to your faithful promise and the humble longing of my will, grant to all who read this account in humility, gratitude for your generosity, compassion for my unworthiness and compunction at their own progress. Out of the golden censers of their loving hearts may so sweet an odor ascend to you that it may make abundant recompense to you for my every failure of ingratitude and negligence.[21]

Love is the great motive force of the soul. Gertrude offer us a typical example of this fact, alongside the equally intense, expressive testimonies of Bernard, Aelred, Baldwin of Ford, or Gilbert of Hoyland. This goes to show that our own stuttering attempt to say something about the formation of the heart, about teaching people how to love, connects with something that was present in the Cistercian vision of the eleventh and twelfth centuries as a clear, deliberate component, free from the false modesty that, today, poisons our attempts to love and to teach others how to love. The founders of Cîteaux were known as lovers: lovers of God, lovers of the brethren, lovers of the place. It can truly be said that the Cistercian experience is never without an affective dimension. Of course, Gertrude's affective language, strong, free, almost brazen as it is, presupposes a radical purification of faith. It no less presupposes the utter liberty of a heart free from the enthrallment of earthly mendacity; a crystalline purity of feeling, released from vain complacence. Indeed, the more Gertrude grows in spiritual stature, the more acute is her awareness of her sinfulness. It is with a sense of being infinitesimally small before God that she clings to him with a passion that can be consummated only in a kiss, in a profound, living union with the Source of all good.

A Pedagogy of Charity

In order to arrive at a healthy affective life, it is useful to be aware of a few factors, in themselves quite banal, that are no doubt common to most religious or monastic communities. By naming them, we will find it easier to point out the right way to follow. As our own community looks back over the road we have traveled, we can identify many an Augustinian *felix culpa* that retrospect helps us to define.

The first obstacle presents a real hindrance to affective maturing. It consists in a lack of inward cohesion, a lack of common judgment on the part of the community, often caused by the tendency of fraternal relationships to be arrested at a superficial level, or by habits of murmuring and destructive criticism. We know how sternly Saint Benedict condemns the vice of murmuring. He considers it to be a source of division in community, irreducibly breaking up fraternal communion.

For a person's affectivity to mature in a healthy way, meanwhile, a certain number of conditions need to be in place: genuine unity within the community; the existence of a common vision, constantly and passionately sought for through community dialogue and the banishment of selfish individualism; a real love, based on truth and forgiveness, for the community and every sister within it. Above all, the community needs to be united around the authority of the house, holding the person who for it represents Christ in genuine and mature affection.

Especially important within the cohesion of the wider community, as a touchstone of authenticity, is a cordial, trusting, mutual recognition among people who belong to the same monastic "generation," that is, among the sisters who entered the monastery together and together went through the stages of formation. If such recognition does not take place, experience has shown us that it is difficult to bring about a positive, heartfelt, faithful integration into the wider community. Instead, small clans are constructed based on ambiguous affinities or dubious alliances.

If relationships within the community are marked by affective poverty, we begin fatally to resolve the problems of our own lives or of the monastery itself outside the community, among persons who have no share in the common life, be they confessors, spiritual directors, friends, or even our own family. We feel free to ask them whatever we like and to tell them whatever we like. In such a scenario, the community has ceased to be a life-giving environment; it is no longer the environment to which we refer to ourselves as persons. Indeed, we may start feeling that our conscience is violated and our liberty compromised if attempts are made to involve the authority of the house in assessing the behavior of the community or of individuals within it. Our way of relating to the superior thus assumes a merely formal character. It is limited to requests for permission, to dealing with various needs, without having any impact on our formation and growth as persons.

What is at stake here? We must learn to walk a path of faith, seeking clarity and fidelity with regard to our vocation, while at the same time letting our heart be profoundly engaged. It is not enough to pursue simply the holy, vertical striving toward God, sustained by liturgical prayer and the generous fidelity of strict observance. Certainly, this striving characterized the generations of monks and nuns that preceded our own. These people came from a social and family setting that was marked by simplicity and unity. Values such as loyalty, fidelity, and gratitude (especially with regard to superiors) were still given much importance. Starting from the postwar years, we have found ourselves faced with a world that is much more torn, engaged in radical transformations. This world has dealt a death-blow to fidelity and its accompanying ideals. It has stimulated reactive behavior and habits of furious criticism even though it gives the appearance of remaining anchored in a certain obstinate conformism, nurturing nostalgia for formal perfectionism and private devotions within its strongly individualistic orientation.

It is beyond doubt that those earlier years of intense labor
yielded many saints; yet in many communities of both men
and women there was a keen sense that something was
missing: a healthy flow of affectivity, genuine integration
of individuals in the community, a spirit of faithful mutual
acceptance and affection. Those were the days in which
communities were accustomed to the severe judgment of
proclamation in the Chapter of Faults, a practice that did not
help to bring out and affirm the positive potential that was
certainly present in each brother or sister, nor did it do much
to unite the community in a common judgment and vision. It
would appear that the heart remained unengaged. We have
already referred to the vertical striving toward God through
observance and liturgy. The horizontal striving, meanwhile,
was less in evidence. Slight attention was given to the positive embrace of one's own community and to nurturing the
sense that dedication to God necessarily implies dedication,
in faith and love, to the "little church" made up by one's own
community. Everyone knew that the cross is made up of two
axes and that the vertical axis must be fixed to the horizontal
axis if the redemptive offering is to be consummated. Only
thus can we bring to birth the eucharistic dimension of life in
common that is called *communion*. Everyone knew this. But
it was not yet obvious how to translate this knowledge into a
concrete way of living together.

The historical transformation of our own community was
at times characterized by keen awareness of these difficulties,
but this fact never led us to reject our past or to stigmatize it
as something negative. It is the task of every community to
draw from its own history—even from those aspects that may
appear most problematic and least positive—the outline for
the way ahead. Our past, the grace that is alive in tradition, is a
tremendous school in which to begin a pedagogical process fit
to strengthen the bonds of love among ourselves in affection
and mutual giving and receiving. By reflecting on our own
history, we have come to recognize certain stages on this path,
and these have been verified in our encounter with the young

who are currently in formation. For being very simple, these stages are prodigiously fruitful.

Stages of Affective Growth

Affective Engagement

On the level of pedagogy, which remains our principal concern, we have sought above all to accept and carry, with serenity, respect, and hope, all the stages of affective growth gone through by the young women who have flocked to our monastery. Let us consider the classical example of affective dependence on the novice mistress. It represents an inevitable, necessary stage that can neither be repressed nor ignored nor condemned. Rather, it must be oriented and purified. It can be directed in a positive way to help a person pass from a merely formal attachment to the life of the community to a sense of belonging that, because it engages the affections, is charged with conviction. In being purified, the heart is enlarged. Such a process only works within the dynamic of affectivity, only, that is, insofar as a person experiences affection. The heart must be committed and engaged. Only in this way do destructive mechanisms of possessiveness, jealousy, and aggression come to the fore. Affection brings them out and unmasks them. It likewise calls forth the qualities of generosity and dedication, from which a growth in love can proceed. The pedagogy we have adopted, then, is twofold. On the one hand, we unconditionally approve each individual's rich affective potential as it begins to express itself. On the other hand, we battle against all those mechanisms of human selfishness that neutralize and paralyze love by suffocating the breath of truth and freedom that is indispensable for true, constructive affection.

Projection and Identification

The second inevitable stage involves a tendency to identify closely with the person we first meet on entering the monastery, the person who looks after *me*. On the part of an immature candidate, it can unleash all sorts of love-hate mechanisms that turn the person with whom we identify into a sort of coatrack. Onto this object I demandingly pile all the qualities I deem desirable in a person charged with formation. At the same time, I unrealistically remove the limitations I am unprepared to admit. I either rejoice in my coatrack or am scandalized by it, according as it corresponds or not to my dreams and demands. Our monastic pedagogy has never sought to cancel out this inevitable process of projection. But it has always underlined the vital importance of two terms that are crucial in confronting it: the *word* on the one hand, *truth* on the other. What we try to do is this: to shift the candidate's attention from a *person* to the *word of that person*, letting the young understand that the dynamic of projection must turn into *fidelity* to the word we receive: that is, fidelity to the demands of obedience and fraternal correction, in an openness to accept the judgment of others on our behavior and on our vision of things and of life.

In formation of this kind, affection, memory, attention to the word, and fidelity to direction join together as so many elements played out in concrete reality. Beyond the bounds of authentic reality there can be no real commitment, only the ambiguous construction of empty relationships. Once we live within this kind of reality, we pass beyond the idea of the coatrack. We accept the word that is addressed to us not for the strengths and weaknesses of the person who speaks it, not motivated by sympathy or hostility, but trusting in the authority to which God has entrusted us, by which he lets his will for us be expressed.

Childish Regression

This too is an inevitable stage, almost invariably a feature of the clash between our previous world and the reality of the new, monastic world we enter. Having been used to living autonomously, independently, affirming ourselves, we suddenly experience religious dependence and the surrender of our own will to the will of God, mediated for us by the person who guides us and by the structures that carry us. The regression that ensues feeds with tremendous urgency our need for attention and our yearning to be understood. It produces dangerous frustration when we do not meet the affective concern to which we feel entitled. For some time, infantilism was spoken of as a tendency that must be fought and replaced by virility. This kind of discourse presupposed a stern system of defense that rejected all expressions of affectivity as signs of perilous weakness in a human person. Personally, I think it preferable to use this inevitable regression as a means of facilitating access to a positive sense of need. If we admit it humbly, it opens us to the grace of dependence, to the gift of knowing how to make requests instead of demands, to the experience of spiritual poverty, to the grateful recognition of mercy received. Oriented well, regression can give access to the Gospel beatitude of the poor in spirit, to the maturity of the publican who, aware of needing mercy and pardon, asks for pity and so leaves the temple a just man. In this way we fight against the proud self-sufficiency that rises up in judgment of the weaknesses of others while forgetting the need we all have for the brethren's compassion.

Forming People to Love in Truth

It is a great pedagogical challenge to form a person to affective fidelity, to an ascesis of friendship in an ongoing process of conversion. Only too easily our claims to autonomy conceal themselves behind an outward discourse on charity, even using this cover as a way of justifying unfaithfulness, to cover up faults, or to provide hypocritical excuses for our own arbitrary behavior. By placing the discourse on charity above any and all observance (on the grounds that the commandment to love is the first and the greatest), we can, in fact, risk nurturing ambiguities and misunderstandings. This kind of discourse is untrue, for in order to subsist charity *needs* fidelity and truth. Charity can never build on unfaithfulness. Mutual affection never grows out of noncompliance and irregularity. Either we love for the good of the other, for the good of the community, to affirm the gift of a vocation that we and all our brothers or sisters have received, or we love for our own sake and profit. In the latter case, love soon fizzles out and we are left with nothing but arid selfishness.

How well we know the weariness and grief caused, for instance, when in the name of charity we compromise silence or when we resign ourselves to the murmuring of another because we fancy that fraternal affection must provide an outlet for just about anything. How well we know the falsity of affective attachments that aim solely at creating connivance for convenience's sake. How well we know the kind of virtuousness that provides a facade while never confronting the truth within, and thus has nothing to do with love.

There is nothing new about these realities. They will be there in the future too, for unfaithfulness ever finds a nest in the human heart. However, the pedagogical process of our community has led us, again and again, at least to call an imbroglio cloaked by "charity' by its true name. Thus we have discovered the *true* face of love. True love builds up the common good and the unity of the community. It consolidates our bonds with our superiors and creates communion among the sisters in a constant momentum of conversion.

We have spoken of a kind of pedagogy that gives us access to our heart of hearts. It enables us to express genuine tenderness and fidelity without falling into the ambiguous waters of possessive individualism and exclusive friendship. We could give many other examples, some of them no doubt even more significant and important. But these modest examples drawn from our own history, from our journey on the path of love, can at any rate be indicative of a greater reality.

Finding a Method, Staking Out a Path

The method required for this kind of formation always, inevitably, and fundamentally presupposes an intense formation to the life of prayer, both personal and liturgical. It presupposes the patient labor of the heart as it slowly learns to listen to the God who is present in our heart of hearts by his Word and Eucharist, by the sacraments and *lectio divina*, by the word spoken to us through the life of our local community-church and the teaching of the superiors who guide it.

The dimension of listening belongs intrinsically to the education of the heart. We must strive to experience an authentic encounter with Him who is the Sum of our life, the Wherefore of existence, the ultimate Meaning of everything. An encounter of this kind calls for openness, interiorization, and silence. Interior silence is truly love's own space. If this personal, intimate, definitive encounter does not occur, the heart will never know what it means to be attracted by someone for whom it is worth living and dying. It will never know the transfigured experience of Tabor that makes us embrace the disfigured face of the Crucified One with an equal excess of love. The encounter takes place in a profound experience of waiting that is charged with love and humility. It opens our heart to receive and perceive the visit of the Word, whose Presence never betrays the expectations of one who does not seek empty consolations but endures in the solitude that must accompany this waiting in pure faith. In this silence, the "rumination of the Word" dear to the Fathers emerges from memory; our *lectio* gushes forth in words of prayer that accompany our day and color it with true, pulsating affection.

Our affection for Christ is the source of whatever affection it is given us to experience within our community. I am not able to love anyone at all if the love of Christ has not first wounded my heart, laying it open to an immense, gratuitous, concrete, and crucified embrace that encompasses every brother or sister. The wounded hands of Saint Francis of Assisi teach us a great deal about his vocation to be a "friend to all." One who has encountered Love, loves.

If this affective force is translated into real experience, in our individual lives and in the life of our community, it may issue in a method of encounter through dialogue with each member of our community. By this means, based on an affection that savors of Gospel truth, we seek oneness and real communion.

Now that this fundamental premise has been articulated, I shall turn to speak of the development of *dialogue* as a pedagogical tool in teaching people how to love. We must consider its role especially in the two fundamental stages of formation, the novitiate and the monasticate. What marks this dialogue? It pursues unity and truth among the persons who participate. While being sincere and deep, it refers to the authoritative word of the superior as a determining factor in the dialogue itself. It makes no sense to carry on a dialogue based merely on a vague, sentimental wish to be together, but it is always enriching and life-giving to conduct a shared search for the common good. This dialogue can be pursued in smaller contexts, too, when sisters meet to clear up a conflict or to make arrangements for a collaborative project. It aims above all to stimulate in individuals a permanent attitude of listening and an openness to being corrected. It aims to help them overcome aggression, self-defence, and self-justification in order to embrace that mutual affection which sustains the process of conversion. The experience of such dialogue has at Vitorchiano generated a desire to continue nurturing the positive harmony of the generational groups that have come through the novitiate and monasticate together. They remain coherent units also after their launch into the larger context of the great monastic family. Thus we have seen the birth of several generational groups with attractive biblical names: the Ark, the Remnant of Israel, the Promise, Zion, and Emmaus. Naturally, the rate of encounter is reduced with time, in the measure of increased work commitments and the responsibilities people assume in the adult community. And it is hard work, sometimes, to carry on with the commitment of regular meetings, to find a time that suits everyone, to vanquish the temptation, always there, to withdraw to the sideline, giving priority to encounters that are easier than those with the sisters in whose company we have grown up, who know everything about us, who see very well what we are living through, and who do not hesitate to nail our infidelities to the cross.

Another dialogical tool is our practice of Revision of Life in the Workplace. The point of it is to generate a will to collaborate and share in responsibility, in harmony with the sister who, right next to me, carries with me the burden of meeting the community's needs, the labor of service. This passion for communion has always engaged the sisters who carry responsibility for a given sector of work, in order that their responsibility does not become a little kingdom apart but remains at the service of the community. It has also engaged the sisters whose job it is to collaborate in a minor capacity, not only in order to nurture shared responsibility and complementarity, but even more in order to favor thoughtful, affectionate attention with regard to each sister, especially for the sister who may be less able or more difficult or who tires more easily but who has an equal need to feel needed and to be included in the enterprise of work.

The pedagogical tool par excellence in this realm of dialogue has been the establishment of faithful, frequent, authentic exchange with the authority of the house. It gives each sister an opportunity to put her own life to the test. For the youngest sisters, the authority will be represented by the person they have dealings with in formation when they enter the monastery, in other words, the novice mistress. For the other sisters, it is the abbess, to whom the final word belongs in any case, who represents authority. Alongside individual encounters, we give ample space and attention to discernment in the Pastoral Council, or even at the level of the community. This discernment is carefully listened to and evaluated. It has made us appreciate the decisive importance of the word of the community-church for each person within it, since it is this word that binds individuals, in faith and affection, to the community as a whole.

Precious above all else are the unity, the intrinsic faithfulness, and the harmony by which all the persons who look after formation are at one in a communion of judgment, vision, and method. Such unity is the true source of affective growth for individuals. How often we have heard our young sisters utter the now famous phrase: "What helps me most is to hear that the Abbess and Novice Mistress are really of one mind!"

At this point we ought perhaps to formulate some kind of conclusion, but I think it preferable to leave this chapter open-ended. Its subject matter is too vast, and our treatment of it has been too incomplete. It needs to be complemented by reflection born of each individual formator's personal experience. Let us, though, hold on to the meaning and importance of affective engagement. It must play its part if we are to form people in a way that enables them to love, both for the sake of their individual growth and in our effort to develop the unity of our community.

Monasticism and Mission

To speak of mission is to speak of what it is to be Catholic, of the dynamic of expansion that is intrinsic to Gospel witness. When I believe in something, I pass it on. When something is supremely important in my life, I bear witness to it. When I know what gives meaning to my existence, I speak of it again and again with words, with gestures, with my entire life. The missionary character of monasticism articulates our passion for the conversion that our monastic life proposes. We wish it to be offered to all the peoples of the earth. We wish to spread faithfulness to a charism that has motivated our own hope, anchoring us at the heart of the Church, blending us together in community, in a living experience.

For this very reason, an authentic monastic mission is rarely born as the project of individuals, although the inspiration to which individuals are subject may well turn out to reveal something important. Normally, the missionary instinct stirs at the heart of a community that listens to the voice of the Spirit and the call of the Church. This call enters into the fabric of the community's thinking and exchange. No one is left out; everyone shares in it. It takes flesh when we place ourselves entirely at God's disposal, an attitude that is itself a gift of God, always given within the context of prayer, obedience, and clear-sighted community decisions that rule out subjective and merely adventurous enterprises.

A nun should always be ready to leave for the mission, that is, for a foundation. She should likewise always be ready to stay at home. Everything depends on what obedience requires of us. However, whether she is sent off or stays at home, every

105

sister is called to assume the labor and the risk brought on by missionary expansion. At the outset, the founding community will certainly have the impression of becoming poorer. In reality, though, it receives even more than it gives.

The sisters who remain at home are called to broaden their ecclesial and cultural horizon. They are called to focus on essentials, making their own examination of conscience before the radical form of life the foundresses are called to embrace. They are called to grown-up generosity in facing unforeseen situations of difficulty that are caused, whether at work or in community living, by reduced personnel. A foundation calls for a fresh start. It sometimes involves pain. It often involves us in the concrete challenge of plugging holes when sisters leave. Through this experience, the integrity of our vocation is tested and made more profound. It often happens that a mission in foreign lands evangelizes the soil of the motherhouse.

The sisters who depart will face the manifold challenges of monastic expansion and the need for infinite cultural adjustments. Nonetheless, the essential character of monastic transmission must remain integral, deep, and clearly recognizable. At all times, the fundamental components of the Benedictine experience must remain tangibly, definitely in evidence. I refer to the community's clearly coenobitic lifestyle under a rule and an abbot, the *Opus Dei* that imposes its rhythm on time, *lectio divina*, vigils, simplicity, and solitude. The most significant inculturation called for is without doubt that of remaining faithful to our own monastic charism, while listening attentively to what the local Church is telling us. Yes, inculturation does mean attention to the riches of local life and culture. But even more fundamentally it means introducing the perennial *newness* of the Gospel into local culture as a living, loving leaven. By this criterion we shatter any false appearances of inculturation that in reality turn out to work against the Gospel.

Let us take liturgical, choral prayer as an example, and let us imagine its impact in an Asian cultural setting. The praying experience of a Benedictine liturgy frees people from the flight away from existential reality that characterizes certain meditational experiences in their quest for immovable, disincarnate abstraction, likewise from a form of concentration that aspires to absolute self-control, from experiences, that is, hardly compatible with the mystery of incarnation within which we live and move.

Another example might be the respect for manual work that is typical of the Cistercian tradition. In environments marked by inflexible divisions of mutually exclusive classes and casts, where the disdain shown to peasants menaces even religious life with attitudes of elitism, it makes a great impression to see the living witness of a nun who works as the poor do in order to earn her daily bread. Such a testimony is pregnant with humility and Gospel truth. By sharing with and serving the local population, a monastic community can help to eliminate distinctions of classes and culture, to overcome divisions between servants and masters, bearing witness to fraternal charity among the children, all equal, of the one God. This is perhaps the most tangible form of cultural integration. The sisters of our own foundations have often written home telling of the amazing spectacle they present to locals as they take their equal share, quite simply and with up-rolled sleeves, in the construction of the monastery or in work on the fields. When it further happens that the locals see how a loving, attentive affinity can grow out of such simple sharing in their simple life, when they receive help in their need—after a flood, say, or an earthquake, or some illness—a new kind of friendship and respect is born, an evangelical sense of the Christian notion that all people are equal since all people are children of God. A communion that comes about in this way is by all accounts much more profound than a simple adaptation to local culture.

After our first Italian foundation at Valserena in 1968, our community saw the genesis, in the 1970s and 1980s, of a new sensibility to mission. We embraced a new openness to the work of expansion in the Church and in the world. Our foundations have for us been a way of responding to the explicit call of the Lord. Life-giving fruitfulness is born from Christ's words, "Go into all the world and proclaim the good news to the whole creation" (Mark 16:15), a fruitfulness rooted in the blood of the martyrs and the offering of the saints. Meanwhile, the Second Vatican Council, whose vision was at the time taken ever more to heart and pondered in the Order, established the theological basis for the missionary effort of both the universal and the monastic Church.

The Doctrinal Basis

Let me now bring to the fore some thoughts from Father Joseph Aubry, SDB, who offers us a splendid synthesis of the missionary character of consecrated persons according to the teaching of the Second Vatican Council:

> Every Christian personally participates in the Easter mystery by virtue of the baptism that establishes him as a member of Christ, son of the Father and brother to all other Christians. But he no less participates in Pentecost by virtue of the anointing with chrism that establishes him as a perfect member of the Church, a public, official witness to Christ, an active, effective worker in the mission of the Church through the power of the same Holy Spirit (*cf. Lumen Gentium* 11a, 30, 33b). *A fortiori*, Christians who are not only baptized and anointed with chrism but also consecrated receive from the Lord and from the Church, on the day of their profession, a more explicit mandate to work for the progress of the Kingdom. [. . .] There is no consecrated person, not even the most austere contemplative (*cf. Lumen Gentium* 46b), who is not called to build up the Church, who is not "sent into the world" as having a part to play in the Church's essential task of being an efficacious sign of God's saving Love for the world. [. . .] This apostolic gift of self is related to the offering made of oneself to God. It springs forth from this consecration and

is its indispensable expression. It is far from the Council's mind that one could really give oneself to a Personal God without pouring oneself out to a like extent for the salvation of the world, just as Jesus did when he expressed his infinite love for the Father in his heroic fidelity as obedient Servant for the salvation of humankind.[1]

More recently, the Church has expressed her thinking on this subject even more clearly. In the working document that prepared the Synod of Bishops on consecrated life and its mission in the Church and in the world (1994), we find several statements that, faithfully echoing the Council documents, rehearse the indissoluble bond that unites the Church's mission to her nature:

> We shall truly understand the Church if we do no separate her mystery from her mission, which is not an added extra but a part of her most intimate nature. [. . .] Even as Christ, consecrated and sent into the world, made of all his life a redemptive mission, so consecrated persons, who are called to reproduce the image of the Firstborn through the agency of the Spirit, must, by analogy, make of their entire life a mission. (n. 61f.)

The document insists on the intrinsic link between vocation, consecration, and mission. The unity springs from the doctrine of creation and incarnation, mysteriously adapted one to the other, each presupposing the other. Insofar as consecration signifies a new creation by grace, it is impossible to conceive of it as not expressing itself as mission, as spreading, that is, the grace of incarnation and the prophetic message of the Kingdom. Institutes devoted exclusively to a life of contemplation get a special mention: "In the institutes dedicated wholly to contemplation, the contemplative life itself constitutes mission" (n. 63). The presence of such institutes in every part of the earth makes manifest the spousal, praying face of the Church, though it is true to say that, wherever they are found, the Spirit causes their life of contemplation to shine over the

entire world for the salvation of humankind. At the Synod
itself, Saint Thérèse of Lisieux and Blessed Maria Gabriella of
Unity were called to mind on account of the vastness of their
missionary zeal, though this was lived out in hidden fidelity
to their contemplative life.

Attention is further drawn to the prophetic role of consecrated life in the context of mission. Consecrated life is by
its nature prophetic because it rejects worldly idols and affirms the primacy of the Beatitudes and the finality of human
existence. It constitutes a mystery. As such, it poses serious
questions for people of every culture, every epoch, and every
social standing. Why is it prophetic, this testimony brought
by consecrated life? It is prophetic because, instead of envisaging earthly gains, it looks toward the ultimate meaning of
human life.

Already at the Congress of Benedictine Abbots in 1987,
Dom Bernard de Soos, then president of the Alliance Inter-
Monastères, asked why monasticism had delayed for so many
centuries before owning its call to missionary expansion:

> If the Church is essentially a missionary Church, all the
> energy of the Church must contribute to the common enter-
> prise of the missions, and the universal Church is directly
> responsible for the primary evangelization of the nations. It
> follows that the monk must acquire and nurture this sense
> of universal responsibility. The very first monks do seem to
> have been inhabited by this kind of zeal. When somebody
> asked Pachomius why he had become a monk, Pachomius
> answered: "In order to save the world." Or think of Antony
> rushing to Alexandria to sustain the Church as soon as he
> learned of the ravages wrought by heresy. Against this back-
> ground, we could cast our eye over monastic history in the
> centuries leading up to our own and ask whether Western
> monks have in fact maintained this sense of responsibility?
> Why, in the wake of the great discoveries made by sea, did
> we wait three or four centuries before going out to India
> or the West Indies? Why was it a pope, Pius XI, and not a
> monk or nun who found a solution to the problem posed by

monastic life in mission territories, by asking monks to go there, not so much to work as missionaries, as simply to get on with their monastic life? I shall never forget the words addressed to me by the archbishop of a city in India whose guest I was in January 1986: "Ah, you are a Benedictine! You are only fifteen centuries too late!"[2]

Another very interesting and profound perspective on this subject is provided by Dom Plácido Álvarez: "Foundations have at times been conceived of as an option or a problem, as something which is not essentially linked to our monastic life. Here we think of them as a necessity and a grace, as something which is intimately related to our life as a church, as a Christian community."[3] As far as Vitorchiano is concerned, the hard work and the sadness involved in every new departure notwithstanding, we have always considered our foundations as a specific response to the will of God, as a grace of vocation in the Church that is intimately tied up with the future of the founding community. We have thought in terms of a response, not in terms of an option, for monastic foundations form a part of the mission of the Church, and it is the Church that calls. Indeed, a foundation only makes sense in terms of a desire to see the monastic church present in every human reality, to give the face of the Church that dense character of spousal love that defines contemplative living (*cf. Ad gentes* 18): "The presence of a Cistercian contemplative community in the local churches is part of their fullness and part of the fullness of the Cistercian church itself."[4]

These are but a few elements of doctrine representing, I would say, the features that have most commonly formed the consciousness of our community. By the grace of God, they have canceled out any search for novelty or adventure, defining the experience of foundation as a response in faith to the call of God and of the Church. Subsequent to the brief wave of euphoria that followed the foundation of Valserena (*Elle est partie en flèche!* said our then Abbot General Ignace Gillet: "It was off like a shot!"), our enterprises of foundation have largely been marked by pain and by faith. The separation causes pain. Faith grows through the hard work of integration into a great unknown. From the point of view of culture, environment, language, economy, and social setting, *everything* is unknown and demanding. Huambo, our house in Angola, can stand as the ultimate witness to this process of crucifixion, so characteristic of the labor of foundations throughout the filiation of Vitorchiano.

Key Issues a Foundation Must Face

A foundation will always represent a drawn-out, difficult process of conversion and a fresh owning of our vocation. Several elements combine to reveal challenges in the common life that did not, perhaps, seem quite so acute in the larger, secure setting of the motherhouse. Among these elements are the small size of the founding group; the entirely new environment; the hard work of forming a monastic settlement that, at the outset, is always precarious and lacking in definition. The foundation has to be remade, as it were, every day. Other challenges that make themselves felt might be the difficulty the foundresses have in forming a unity among themselves, in accepting one another, and in showing loyalty to a new superior. There will inevitably be differences of opinion regarding buildings to be put up or structures to be laid down. One is up against the hard work of getting on in a new language and in an environment that is totally unknown. The sisters may feel painfully weighed down by solitude or homesickness. There is a natural anxiety connected with the search for sustaining, sustainable work.

To these difficulties of the early years, others are slowly added later, such as when the foundation little by little requires the foundresses to disappear from view and make way for new generations of local sisters, who must be allowed to express themselves and take charge of administration. At the same time, the process of formation will still have great need of the foundresses, not so much of their teaching of theory as of the example of their lives.

The particular energy of foundation, at first condensed in a yes of faith to the call of the Lord and of the Church, necessarily expresses itself in a different way when translated into real experience. In the unfamiliar context of a foundation, many aspects of life will seem different from what they were like at the heart of the motherhouse, defined as it was by established structures, rich in possibilities and human potential. I shall now bring to light some of the criteria that have helped us deal with the key problems posed by a foundation.

Creating Unity among the Foundresses

From the moment it is first constituted at the heart of the motherhouse, we have always tried to construct this unity on the basis of conversations and exchanges on the fundamental values of the monastic calling. It is not enough to build on natural sympathies, similarities of temperament, or the facile enthusiasm produced by novelty.

Praying the Divine Office in the Language of the Foundation

We have always considered the great cycle of liturgical prayer as the primary, undisputed source of unity in the group. The rock on which we seek to create a new church in unity has always been the foundresses' practice of praying together. While still in the motherhouse, they begin to celebrate the Divine Office as a group, just as they will do once the foundation has been made, in the language of that new place. They share in the effort to create a liturgy that is adequate and beautiful. It is by prayer, above all by *liturgical* prayer, that they will find the resources they need to face difficulties, loneliness, the hard work of creating unity, and cultural adaptation. This prayer is the first and primary gesture of communion performed by the foundresses once they arrive in the land to which God has called them. Thus the attention given to initial efforts has always been blessed by the Lord, even as it has been a source of blessing for the founding community, which sees a new praying community coming into being in its midst. Certainly, the liturgy can also be a source of conflicts and squabbles. The temptation of perfectionism is always lurking in the wings. Different sensibilities with regard to taste, rhythm, and ways of doing things can be difficult to put up with. But this remains a necessary starting point.

Accepting the New Superior

There is no standard way of preparing the sister called to exercise the service of authority, for it is a delicate thing to guide others by serving, to assume responsibility while valuing the contribution of all, to carry the full weight of circumstances without letting this weigh the little community down, instead making constant efforts to bring about collaboration and an experience of complementarity that is intelligent and cordial, so that each sister in equal measure feels involved and responsible. A community is never helped to grow toward freely sharing responsibility if the superior shows herself to be authoritarian, impatient, or anxious, or if she demands, as if by right, to be understood. This running-in phase is difficult also for the other members of the group. They easily run the risk of sliding into conflicts over superficial matters, of stressing the limitations of the other sisters or of the superior, forgetting that, for unity to be born, we need above all to affirm the community and the authority that God is pleased to ordain. Affirmation of this kind remains the royal road by which we attain the highest good of obedience, the criterion of truth by which our monastic calling is measured.

Shared Responsibility in Initial Decision Making

Co-responsibility is a way of building, a way of working, a way of exercising leadership. What I refer to is not democracy by a sociologist's definition. That would simply be unhelpful. I refer, rather, to a harmony that is arrived at through dialogue, in search of the common good. This harmony expresses itself in the sisters' ability to participate responsibly in the running of the house, giving their best and growing through vigilant attention to the life of the community. A foundation needs *all* the resources of mind, heart, competence, and dedication of *all* the foundresses if it is to live out in fullness the witness that God requires of it. Therefore they must all be prepared to let themselves be used in whatever way necessity dictates, with the heartfelt dedication of persons who know that it is by giving ourselves that we come alive.

Inculturation

Experience has taught us to base the work of inculturation on the criteria of respect, humility, listening, and, most important, on a capacity for wonder before the inexhaustible riches of humanity that God has placed in the midst of his people. Both in the community as such and in the hearts of the foundresses, this dynamic of inculturation creates a space of welcome for the local people, whether they come to visit or are seeking to become part of the monastic community. We want them to feel welcome, understood, embraced, and valued even in their most specific characteristics. A foundation is not about creating a cultural success story. Rather, it affirms our monastic calling, our clinging to the Lord, our passion for the spread of God's kingdom in the place that God gives us, with the resources and modes of expression offered by that place.

Transmitting a Tradition

What is asked of us is to transmit the Cistercian calling in its integrity: the values in which it consists, the structures that define it. Of this we are well aware. In the course of Vitorchiano's missionary experience, we have never dreamed of inventing a new kind of monasticism in order to adapt to particular socio-geographical circumstances. It is by remaining faithful to the patrimony we have received that we become apt to discern the newness of local conditions, the home-grown genius, and to graft this onto the ancient trunk of tradition in a fruitful, original way. This is what experience has taught us.

Further, what local vocations seek is the transmission of a tradition that is authentic and true, genuine and integral, able to insert the life of the fledgling community into the pulsating life of the Order, in faithfulness to origins that, seeming at once remote and close, are a wellspring of grace for each individual vocation.

Also important is the transmission of real love for the founding house. The point of this is not that the foundation should pursue a passive, senseless imitation of the way things are done at home. The point is to make it clear how precious it is to have an origin, to have been generated. What is the meaning of sonship? It is to have life-giving roots from which we can grow in hope and thankfulness for the life we have received. Nothing hampers growth more than a desire to generate oneself from nothing, as if one could emerge in autonomous blossoming without recognizing the need for the life-giving trunk which makes the novelty of birth possible.

The transmission of a life, a charism, is always the fruit of unity. It springs from the love that circulates in the community, pouring forth onto the young in formation as a generative force, as a pledge of their future growth. And so we find ourselves facing, ultimately, the hard question that never ceases to challenge us: Is the love, the mutual acceptance, tolerance, pardon, and friendship that circulate in the veins of our community such that our life truly communicates the love of Christ to those who enter it?

The style of monastic pedagogy we have received suggests yet another aspect of the transmission of life, namely, the commitment of the foundresses to pass on a taste for self-knowledge in truth. I refer to that depth of monastic humility that makes a person glad to be called into question, grateful to be corrected, committed to forgiveness and continuous reconciliation without invoking the privileges of age or position. A person like this is apt to inspire confidence. She is pleased to listen to and learn from the postulant most recently arrived, open to the riches of humanity and culture brought to the monastery from the soil on which it stands.

The Grace of Mission

What, then, flows back into the pedagogy of the founding house from this experience of mission? I can only repeat what I have already said: there is always great grace in store for the monastery that founds, a grace that touches the mature sisters, certainly, but even more profoundly those who are still young in monastic life. It is a grace above all of universality, of catholicity: "This characteristic of universality which adorns the people of God is a gift from the Lord Himself. By reason of it, the Catholic Church strives constantly and with due effect to bring all humanity and all its possessions back to its source in Christ, with Him as its head and united in His Spirit" (*Lumen gentium* 13). In the article already cited, Dom Plácido Álvarez noted that:

> In any case, some may think that the data presented here
> [on the distribution of monasteries in different parts of the
> world] is irrelevant, that it affects little or nothing our com
> munity life, as an Order or as individual communities. We
> think, however, that to the degree that we limit our par
> ticipation in this grace, to that same degree we diminish in
> spirit, and it is not simply a question of more or less monas
> teries in more or less different places. What is involved here
> is the vigor of our charity, the breadth of our communion,
> and the fullness of our identity.[5]

Dom Plácido goes on to explain that the gift of universality, of catholicity, springs from a communion in charity, from the expansive energy of Christ's love, poured into our hearts by the Holy Spirit. He cites from the Apostolic Exhortation *Evangelii nuntiandi* of Pope Paul VI: "Now, only a Church which preserves the awareness of her universality and shows that she is in fact universal is capable of having a message which can be heard by all, regardless of regional frontiers" (n. 63). Individualism, as we well know, constitutes a festering sore in our coenobitic communities. Individualism is the greatest enemy of universality and ecclesial catholicity. We do not deny this fact, but do we act on it? Often, we do not move beyond the realms of theory and sentiment because the remedy, if we really live it out, requires such radical dispossession in an opening up to others, in an option for sharing, in an intrinsically missionary, outward-going energy.

Since 1968, some sixty sisters have gone out to foundations from Vitorchiano. The founding community, on seeing yet another, competent group of sisters leave, must each time close ranks to face the gaps that ensue. These gaps do not regard numbers only. They are gaps of responsibility, of presence, of that effective, unifying force that builds up the communion of the house. At the same time, the community is always open to welcome the sisters who return, sometimes just for a very short time. It listens to them, embraces them with friendship, sustains the strength they need to continue in their mission. One could imagine Vitorchiano as a kind of gigantic bicycle pump! More important, though, it is a *church* generating children who, invested with life, know how to generate life in their turn.

The body of a Cistercian community is built up through a vital impetus that presses it toward its destiny, which is to become the Body of the Lord, to attain the perfect unity that Christ desires for it. This fullness grows little by little through a mutual exchange of gifts among all those who contribute to the growth in unity. By this bond, no one feels diminished. Everyone is enriched by the gift of everyone else. In the context of mission, one who gives his or her own life will always be gifted, to use a biblical term, with "the heritage of the nations," with the contribution of all peoples: "In other words, the identity of the Order cannot be defined while ignoring the expansive thrust of charity, and what other peoples and cultures have to contribute to it. Our identity is in process."[6] I believe that the missionary dimension of our communities lies profoundly embedded in the Marian charism of Cîteaux, for the maternal heart of Mary has the dimensions of all humanity, of every time and every place. In a meditation for the Nativity of the Mother of God, spoken on 8 September 1964, Pope Paul VI defined the infinite mission of Mary with the following words:

> To our great and ever-new joy, to the enchantment of our souls, Mary, when we look to her, arrests our gaze only so as to point it further ahead, to the miracle of light and life and holiness that by her birth she proclaims and always carries with her: to Christ the Lord, her Son, the Son of God, from whom she receives everything. This is the wonderful play of grace we know as incarnation. Today's feast anticipates it in Mary, the lampstand carrying divine light, the gate by which heaven's footfall approaches earth, the mother who gives human life to God's Word, the advent of our salvation.[7]

Through her, earth crosses the threshold of heaven.

Foundations

In 1993, Dom Armand Veilleux made the following remarks in an article that appeared in the review *Cistercium*:

> According to Cistercian tradition, a community is founded by another community, which passes on to it its own expression of the Cistercian spirit. For a community to work out well and develop normally, it has to be desired and cordially supported by the motherhouse. When a foundation is the personal project of an abbot or a small group of founders without being taken on by the whole community (or at any rate, by a majority), it is unlikely to develop. One could give examples of foundations that did begin as personal adventures yet developed soundly all the same. This, however, is solely due to their having been taken on and adopted by the founding community at a given moment in time.[1]

Our own experience has been very much along these lines. We can only add a few particular insights that have accompanied our community's missionary endeavor. First and foremost, there is the sense of corresponding to a destiny. This sense is based on two convictions.

The first conviction refers to a prophecy of Mother Pia Gullini, the abbess who more than any other left her mark on the community of Grottaferrata and who established the basis for a new way of seeing the Cistercian vocation. She did this by her teaching, by her pedagogical flair, and above all by the solitude of her last years that represented, in her heart of hearts, a secret martyrdom. At a time when the tragic experience of war and the devastation wrought by raging tuberculosis, famine, and misery made the situation of the community especially perplexing, Mother Pia used to say: "I see the monastery as a river of life that branches out and carries water to every side." Her words echoed what had been expressed many years before by Mother Thérèse Astoin, who in 1875 founded Grottaferrata's forerunner San Vito, near Turin, from her French monastery of Vaise. Once, while speaking of the poverty of San Vito, Mother Thérèse wrote: "This house will be the mother of many others." Her prophecy remained buried at the heart of the community. Its significance is certainly relative, but it *has* marked our sense of destiny. Every community has its particular grace. But Vitorchiano also has a prophecy to fulfill.

The second conviction comes from the certainty that monastic life should, by duty and by right, be established in all the countries of the world, since the monastic vocation corresponds to man's natural tension toward the absolute, a tension that finds fulfilment only in God. In every place, witness should be borne to the fullness of the Church's charism and mission. When, in 1989, preparations were made to celebrate the five hundredth anniversary of the evangelization of Latin America, Pope John Paul II gave the following message to the continent's contemplative nuns:

> A multitude of people want to have a place in your hearts, to be spiritually united with you in the hymns and prayers you offer up, never for yourself alone, but for all humanity. You hear the cry of so many brothers and sisters who suffer through being poor and marginalized. Many are the expatriates and refugees; many are those who suffer for knowing neither love nor hope. Many are those who have ceded to evil and have become deaf to any spiritual call; many are those whose hearts are bitter, who are the victims of injustice, subject to the power of the strong. You, on the other hand, draw from your immersion in the mystery of God your characteristic moral fortitude and spiritual strength. Through your prayer, penitence, and life of enclosure, you can make love pour forth from the heart of God, the love

that binds us together as brothers and sisters, reins passions in, and creates a communion of minds that bears fruit in solidarity and Gospel charity. [. . .] The travails of the world, troubled as it is by tensions and conflicts, find an echo in your prayer so that people come to perceive, in the events of their lives, how close at hand is the reality that transcends them and remains forever. In you, meanwhile, all this flows into a straight, luminous trajectory, directed toward God and the brethren. From the vessel of your recollection, the interior riches that fill your soul overflow. In this way, you sow the seed of faith everywhere. You nurture the hope and charity of all the pastoral workers of your dioceses.[2]

The constant influx of new vocations, or rather, of new generations, has always given our community a breath of vitality and youth. It has enabled us to broaden and renew our perspective. It has given us a certain kind of missionary audacity that would have been impossible in a different setting. The abundance of vocations is not only a numerical fact. It stands for a grace of cordial, mutual openness, for an attentive, loving readiness to listen, for the slow transformation of a mind-set, a peaceful, fruitful osmosis. Particularly interesting was the rejuvenation our community experienced in the wake of the years from 1965 to 1970. We were faced with a type of youth that no longer came out of Catholic Action, which for so long had been a strong unifying force among young people, producing many vocations to the religious life. They came, rather, from new Church movements that did not follow previous categories of formation according to division by age and gender, with a firm point of anchorage in parish structures. This new type of youth was unfamiliar, perhaps, with some aspects of the strict structures that had characterized Catholic life before the war, when it was impossible to conceive of any authority apart from the hierarchy, the pope, the bishop, and the parish priest. What these young people had received from the Church were a prophetic charism, a thirst for communion, the strength of proclamation, a passion for bearing witness. In the midst of the breakdown of previously authoritative models and of so many moral, religious, and social values, these young people had found a number of factors to be decisive for their maturing:

1. A clear proposition of Christian living in which the personal and communal encounter with Jesus Christ appeared as the only way to live, as the sole alternative to despair and impending void.

2. An experience that carried its own intrinsic authority, whose sense did not depend on structures but on prophecy, on the integrity of the life it proposed.

3. A generous following of Jesus Christ and of persons who passionately transmit the meaning of life according to the Gospel. From this followed a new mode of relationship and mutual recognition among the young themselves, based on the sense that every aspect of life carries an encounter with Presence and therefore calls for a committed response.

It goes without saying that the burdensome aspects of that difficult time did not simply go away. Perhaps they were even intensified by the shattering of society and of families. We encountered insecurities, affective fragility, unpreparedness for binding decisions, and an allergy to concrete sacrifices, to solitude, and to the humdrum routine of life. Nonetheless, a new strength of authenticity, a new quality of discipleship (a discipleship loved and desired), entered our monasteries, furthering the evolution so clearly proposed to us by our General Chapters. We may list certain tangible consequences of this evolution:

- The monastic community was asked to express what it was about in a clear proposition fit to carry conviction. It was challenged to invest values it had long lived faithfully with new content, not dictated merely by a conformity to observances that could verge on perfectionism,

but tending, clearly and freely, toward an experience of
the living God within the *school of charity* that our Cistercian Fathers so clearly had in mind.

- Superiors were expected to play a clear role in the spiritual direction of the community and in the teaching of
doctrine, with a view to forming a shared mentality from
which faithful, free, grown-up discipleship could grow.

- Fraternal life in community was expected to be marked
by true, solid communion, based on an informed effort of
continuous conversion, a sincere search for the common
good, and a free, visible reciprocity in love, fit to serve
and affirm each sister.

All this prepared the premises and strategies of our experience as a founding house. It chimed in with our community's
special grace, although I should stress that our typical features
have not, in fact, been all that different from the general approach to foundations abroad in the Order as a whole.

The invitation to assume the responsibility for a foundation
has always come to us from the Church and from the Order.
The community has thus tried to respond to the Lord's call,
not to elaborate a project on the basis of its own insights or desires. A vocation always calls for a response of faith, a humble
entry into the missionary dimension of the Church, a personal
investment in her universal proclamation to all nations.

It has happened that our actual experience has not entirely
corresponded to the premises outlined above. Still, they have
been a kind of model for our every missionary effort, condi-
tioning the evolution of the community in opening up to the
possibility of foundation and engaging it viscerally in the
process of generating life, preparing it for the costly but fruitful experience of giving birth. In order better to see how this
evolution came about, we may refer to a few facts from our
history. The evaluation I am about to give will no doubt be
very partial, an account, really, of what I personally and our
community as a body have lived through. As for the history

that continues to unfold in our foundations, it belongs totally to each community's special mystery, to each community's special grace.

Our First Foundation: Valserena, Italy (1968)

Vitorchiano's first foundation resulted from an attempt to marshal the excessive size of the community, which had become too large for our buildings to contain: we were ninety-three in the house. At this time, the Order was given to almost feverish experimentation with new solutions. For our part, we were a community without previous experience of foundation and had not yet a very clear idea of what it means to give life to a new monastery or of the patrimony of values we would want to transmit. Our first foundation was thus, at birth, numerically strong, well structured, and endowed with strong monastic values. At the same time, it nurtured a desire for evolution with regard to some details of strict observance that were still in force in the motherhouse. From the outset, this foundation sought to find its own specific way of life, its own grace of growth and life in common, eager to face the novelty and difference that pulsated throughout the Order and the Church.

Valserena immediately stood for an efficient, youthful, sound monastic experience, soon able to be autonomous at every level. Interiorly, too, it showed a distinctiveness that soon made it stand out with regard to its motherhouse. This newness was healthy and necessary, although it probably came about too hastily and with too much independence. As a result, the transmission and integration of life were not as profound as they might have been in the relationship between motherhouse and daughterhouse. Having said which, the influence of Valserena on the founding community has been immense.

Important above all has been a fact we have already referred to: we have found that an enterprise of foundation in which the entire community is involved always gives rise to a new sense of unity. With regard to Valserena, the slight geographical distance between our houses permitted the direct participation of the community as sisters took turns to supervise building work. As a result, we discovered a horizon of shared interest and responsibility thus far unknown.

Valserena's intense commitment to dialogue, its special gift for facing necessary adjustments with great truth and courage, has certainly helped the motherhouse to open up to the value of dialogue, community discernment, and a common search for consensus on fundamental issues. Above all, it has made us ask how we can present and pass on our monastic life. Our first foundation, then, was for us a school of faith, truth, and humility. It has left an indelible mark on our history. Thanks to that experience, we have learned what a foundation is, what it entails, what it calls for.

Our Second Foundation: Hinojo, Argentina (1973)

This experience was very different from the first on account of various factors. First, there was already a foundation of monks in the area, Nuestra Señora de los Ángeles at Azul. Second, when the Order, through the agency of Dom Edmund Futterer and Dom Augustine Roberts, called on us to found, we received ample documentation, as well as a presentation of local conditions prepared by Dom John Eudes Bamberger, then Secretary General of the Order, who had visited the foundations in Latin America. Third, contact with the local Church was established forthwith through Monsignor Marengo, the bishop of Azul. Thus, our foundation at Hinojo was straight away integrated into our basic vocation: to respond to the Lord's call.

Whereas for Valserena the group of foundresses was named from on high shortly before departure, following traditional custom, the choice was now made through a call to the community itself. Sisters who wanted to go were invited to volunteer, although such generous offers were of course later submitted to the evaluation and approval of the community. The group was formed a year before departure. Very soon it began to meet to learn the language of the new country and to put together, as far as possible, its own liturgy so as to share with minimal delay in the prayer of the *Opus Dei* that truly binds a community together. It began the work of integration that must continue for a lifetime.

At this point, it seems worthwhile to say a few words about the meaning of *integration*, since the word, already mentioned in the last chapter, will recur as a leitmotiv in all the foundation stories of our filiation.

It always costs great effort to be integrated into a large group. In a small group, the process happens on different terms. The small group seems to constitute a less anonymous setting than the large community. Thus, we may deceive ourselves into thinking that fraternal relations will be easier and more gratifying. In fact, the small community invariably and mercilessly exposes the limitations and struggles of every individual within it. Whatever problem arises, it is at once evident who is for, who is against. Inevitably, mechanisms of affirmation and defensiveness will come into play when the group is up against a new experience before which all members feel equal responsibility. The superior of the group (not chosen by the group, but named by the motherhouse) for the first time faces the impact of the responsibility she carries and has not yet, obviously, acquired the experience and moral prestige required to provide the service of authority without seeming either authoritarian or weak. When everything is new, everything different, we inevitably feel insecure. We are challenged by the precariousness that belongs to any beginning, by financial difficulties, by the experience of feeling a stranger in local culture. Our fraternal integration into the community is therefore more necessary than ever before. It is also, in certain ways, more difficult than it ever has been. In the context of a foundation, such integration can never be based merely on fidelity to a list of customs and usages. It presupposes responsible fidelity to the spiritual, monastic patrimony of the motherhouse. It calls on us to get to know one another in such a way that we do not shy away from facing the truth about ourselves or about our sisters. We must aim to unite in an effort of mutual acceptance and correction in charity, an effort that requires deliberate choices to be faithful, kind, and friendly. Above all, our integration must be based on loyalty to the appointed superior, as a concrete expression of our loyalty to the Lord.

In order to be integrated into the community, we must *want* to be integrated. We must work at reciprocity in our relationships. It will involve suffering. It will take time. It will happen only through faith. This is the principal lesson taught us by our foundation in Argentina. On that basis we have asked ourselves how real our own integration is, in the setting of our large community.

We have also been given the opportunity to see the relative importance of a number of secondary questions, certain approaches to observance and the common life that do not touch on essentials. And our own capacity for transmission, that is, for maternity, has been put to the test. It is never easy to face the void that ensues and the pain we feel when sisters leave, for when a nun leaves for a foundation she leaves for good. The departure of the foundresses of Hinojo was particularly hard. When they left, Vitorchiano lost its prioress, novice mistress, junior mistress, infirmarian, and wardrobe mistress. In terms of its administration, the community stood before a gaping hole. Yet it remains true that the enterprise of bestowing life helps us to grow quickly. There is an immensely precious grace of growth implicit in the generous service called for to fill gaps left by others, in showing adult readiness to assume new responsibilities, in forgetting one's own needs for the sake of the needs of the house.

From this foundation in particular, we gained the experience of a new kind of relationship with the male branch of the

Order, an experience consolidated by subsequent foundations. Between Vitorchiano and the Italian houses of the male branch there had always been a clear-cut separation, and our relations were limited to the pastoral oversight of our Father Immediate. Through Hinojo, however, we made a new experience of complementarity as the monks of Azul extended their help to us in a way that was cordial and profoundly fraternal. It was a great surprise and an enrichment to find ourselves thus giving a shared witness to the Cistercian vocation.

Inculturation did not present any great difficulty, partly because Italians are, par excellence, a people of poor emigrants who adapt themselves to circumstances, partly because this first contact with Latin America involved a very Europeanized people. No great changes in customs or way of life were required. To speak of inculturation in this context is to speak of humility, of welcoming local vocations with confidence, of valuing what our locality had to offer us, be it simply the immensity of the sky above the Pampas, the sense of friendship and humane relationships that characterizes the Argentines, their great Marian devotion, their history, their political conflicts and economic difficulties. And to this day I ask myself if this is not, indeed, the truest kind of inculturation.

The great lesson of this foundation was the gradual disappearance from view of the founding group as a group of home-grown sisters came splendidly to the fore. All this happened with a peace, a consensus, and a will to communion that I am tempted to qualify as miraculous.

Our Third Foundation: Quilvo, Chile (1981)

The process of making this third foundation resembled that of the second one, although it was facilitated by the experience we had gained as well as by the extraordinary charity and welcome shown us by the monks of La Dehesa, now Santa María de Miraflores, a foundation of Gethsemani that had been present in Chile since 1961.

The process of inculturation required more time and greater attention, since Chile has a clearly defined native culture. Our encounter with local vocations was more laborious. It called for great faith, hope, patience, and discernment. As for the process of integration among the founding sisters, it went deeper and was more painful, perhaps because it was more deliberate and complex. At the same time, it was richer. The group counted sisters of very varied temperament, of keen and critical intelligence, differing in age and monastic experience. They specifically decided to focus more on fostering a spirit of mutual, loving, and patient tolerance than on dialogue and the dialectic exchange of ideas and projects. At the same time, they developed a highly responsible model of collaboration in the areas of work and service, as a result of which this community very quickly became financially self-sufficient. What strikes us in these sisters is their fidelity to the vocational grace received from the motherhouse, alongside a remarkable ability to translate the content of this grace into a response to local need. The inculturation of Quilvo has been fruitful, full of warmth and insight, contributing generously to the life and needs of the local Church. The community's work of formation is lively, competent, and very open to the life of the Order.

Something quite characteristic of our third foundation is its pedagogy of hope, ever able to start afresh after every failure, every trial of ill health, every difficulty whether from within or from without. Its capacity for growth has no equal. As far as Vitorchiano is concerned, it certainly was not easy to see the departure of people who, by their contributions to the sectors of formation, finance, and work, had more or less reconstructed the community when the foundresses of Hinojo left. In return, however, we were enlivened by our third foundation's special ability to reinterpret the patrimony of values it had received in such a profound way, with such freshness of inculturation, while nonetheless transmitting it unambiguously. Vitorchiano itself felt regenerated by this birth.

Our Fourth Foundation: Humocaro, Venezuela (1982)

Of all our foundations, this is the one that clearly stands out. It started life as the personal project of one sister who felt an intense call to the land of Venezuela. This call was motivated by providential encounters. A Venezuelan family made a proposal that was not only very generous but based on a rare understanding of the monastic vocation. We were deeply moved by this proposal, which preceded our foundation in Argentina and so marked the beginning, it would seem, of our looking toward Latin America. However, when the Venezuelan project appeared on the agenda with special insistence, the community was already committed to making its foundation in Chile and could not, in the circumstances, assume a second project. Two sisters were so sure of the goodness of this project that they decided to get on with it all the same. Having obtained an indult of exclaustration, they embarked, between 1978 and 1982, on the hard, painful labor of seeking out a place that would be suitable for constructing a monastery. Through a series of exceptional providential circumstances, their long-suffering search at last led them to settle in the small village of Humocaro, situated within a valley at the foot of the Andes, in the diocese of Barquisimeto. On 2 February 1982, later considered the date of foundation, a first solemn Mass was celebrated by the bishop of Barquisimeto in the small courtyard of Humocaro, which on the occasion served as church. The beginning of this community was precarious and rudimentary though authentically monastic by the hope that suffused it.

A few vocations came to join this uncertain embryonic foundation. Only in 1985 did Humocaro come to be considered a regular foundation from Vitorchiano. It gained status as a community of the Order thanks to the generosity of the Abbey of the Holy Spirit at Conyers, Georgia, in the United States, whose monks regularized the situation that obtained by accepting the immediate paternity of Humocaro. This is the foundation from which we find we have learned most, as is always the case when problems are urgent and difficulties great. Yet again we were confirmed in our insight that a foundation can never be born of a personal project, however lovely, however generous it may be. Only a community can give birth to a foundation, for it transcends persons and pours forth from the heart of the Church.

From Humocaro we have learned that charity remains the one force fit to heal any wound. It ought to embrace the life of all members of the community even in their most questionable and awkward attempts to respond to what they believe is the will of God. It was not easy to move forward from an initially negative judgment, which interpreted the Venezuelan foundation as an "adventure with no substance," toward a will to recover this experience in terms of full recognition. The process gave our community a new breadth of magnanimity, openness, and understanding with regard to something that was utterly *other* yet clearly somehow blessed by God. We learned thereby to regard Vitorchiano as a place of compassion.

We learned that, in order to recover a given history in a positive way, we must walk a path of patience and love. Nothing will make our hearts forget the rich experience of humiliation and hope wrought by the coming to birth of this foundation. As for the sisters who thenceforth, in one group after another, went off to sustain this precarious enterprise with their lives, they set us a rare example by their faith, by their utter fidelity to a task received, and by their love of the *bonus oboedientiae* in acknowledging, in spite of everything, the authority of the foundress. Given the history, place, and structures into which they entered, this deliberate choice was in many respects heroic. In this way Humocaro quickly acquired both a monastic character that was clearly Cistercian and a most regular observance.

In their work, the sisters have served without counting the costs, with creativity and competence, and so we have seen, at last, the building of what may be called a miracle of persistent hope. Today, indeed, Humocaro is a community full of potential and good will. Perhaps it has not yet reached the solidity of the other foundations, but it has acquired a character of its own, a history of suffering and grace, a palpable thankfulness with regard to its motherhouse, and perhaps it is precisely on account of its peculiar development that it is so well inculturated into its Venezuelan setting.

Our Fifth Foundation: Gedono, Indonesia (1987)

This foundation, too, is in many respects distinctive. It was born in response to a request from the Order and exhibits all the charisms that follow the lineage of Vitorchiano, but it has nonetheless followed a unique path.

The difficulties connected with a foundation in the Far East, where there are such great differences of language, customs, mentality, and culture, had already been felt through attempts made by some of our Northern European monasteries of nuns. After much reflection, Dom Frans Harjawiyata, abbot of the Indonesian monastery of Rawaseneng on the Island of Java, together with the then Abbot General Dom Ambrose Southey, decided to move toward a different solution. Their suggestion was to form a group of Indonesian sisters in a European monastery up to the point of simple profession and then to entrust them with the foundation. Our superiors were on the lookout for a monastery that was fairly lively and fairly international to which they could entrust the task of receiving a group of young Indonesian women in order to provide them with an initial monastic formation. Their choice fell on our community. The enterprise soon began to look different on account of the tensions between Indonesian culture and monastic culture, or, rather, between certain aspects of the Indonesian mentality and the Gospel values of the Cistercian vocation.

We often assume that a conflict between cultures arises solely out of the socio-cultural form that has conditioned the development of a form of life in a given continent, in a given geographical position on the map. Sure enough, this remains an important factor. But it often happens that this diversity does not make up the most pertinent aspect of inculturation. As it happens, our Indonesian sisters have been among the most loved, esteemed, and protected members of our community. Their gift for forming relationships, guided by exquisite Asian restraint, made them especially lovable and kind. Our community loved and admired them when they understood how much it cost them to adapt to our climate, our food, and our temperament. One of the first Italian phrases the Indonesian sisters learned was our *Presto! Presto!* The real difficulty of inculturation, meanwhile, took place at the level of conversion, that is, in the passage from a mentality based on culture and social status to a mentality shaped by the Gospel.

The Indonesian cultural schema unquestioningly regards humility as weakness; it never permits the public revelation of the truth about oneself, which is perfectly mastered through a self-control that seeks harmonious coexistence rather than mutual forgiveness and profound integration; obedience rests more on a sense of reverence for the old than on conformity to Christ. Against this background, how strange it seemed to take on humility as a path of truth and in consequence to see the truth about oneself as a point of access to real personal dignity, to embrace obedience as an affirmation of personal maturity and authentic belonging to Christ and the Church, to experience openness to correction as growth, to devote oneself to service as an expression of free and fruitful love. The idea of the Church as ecclesial communion was absent from the traditional Indonesian mentality.

Thus, we had to make a long journey together. The Italian nuns had to make an effort to understand and respect a highly controlled mode of behavior, very different from our own way of relating, which tends to be direct, straight-talking, busy, often instinctive. The Indonesian sisters were, in a way that is typical of the Far East, spontaneously attracted by the contemplative dimension of our life. By attending more to it, we found that it complemented our own natural tending toward action. Above all, we had to provide genuine living space, within our large community, for a small community of eight Indonesian sisters.

On their part, the Indonesian nuns had to accept immersion into a reality that differed from what they were used to, with the difficulties presented by the language, the climate, and the food. Even more essentially, they had to embark on a path of conversion and a drawn-out period of waiting for the fulfillment of their dream, the foundation in Indonesia. For it was obvious from the first that the time of preparation we had first envisaged was insufficient. Monastic formation cannot be rushed. We slowly arrived at the conviction that it would be fitting and prudent that Gedono, too, should follow the criteria for a foundation that normally obtain in the Order, criteria proven by time and experience. It meant helping the Indonesian sisters to continue their cycle of formation up to solemn profession. On that basis they could later face the great trial of a monastic foundation on terms of perfect clarity, with greater religious maturity. We should not forget that the formation of the Indonesian sisters was complicated further by the explicit purpose of their sojourn in Europe, which *was*, after all, a project of foundation. Neither heart nor mind is free to devote itself fully to the chore of conversion when the initiation into monastic life is too intimately tied up with a project of foundation. How often we were uncertain in discernment! What efforts we went to, what a great lesson of purification and prudence we learned together!

Nonetheless, when a period of seven years of formation had been completed, the foundation of Gedono did take place, with eight Indonesian sisters and three sisters from the community of Vitorchiano. Not only was it an Indonesian foundation, something it had been from the start; it was a thoroughly *monastic* foundation manifesting a love of Cistercian tradition, able to express the defining values of our vocation in a way that was clearly Asian and at the same time carried monastic integrity.

It is obvious that we do not reach the end of the path of conversion simply by virtue of making profession. The real testing ground on which Gedono measured how far it had interiorized its vocation was provided by the actual experience of foundation. It revealed the atavistic difficulty of effecting integration among the Indonesian themselves, that is, among the Javanese, Chinese, and those from Sumatra and other islands of the archipelago. Challenging, too, was the integration of the young women who entered Gedono directly and turned out to be very different, both in age and cultural sensibility, from the first eight foundresses. The path of Gospel communion is never predictable. It will always require a death to self, as we embrace the Cross of Christ and remain loyal to the Church, "that they may all be one, as you, Father, are in me and I am in you, that they, too, may be one" (John 17:21). When we persevere, the miracle always happens. From the tears of our dying, the Church, the spouse of Christ, is finally born; the Kingdom of God is born. In his apostolic letter *Tertio millennio adveniente*, Pope John Paul II wrote: "Man achieves this fulfilment of his destiny through the sincere gift of self, a gift which is made possible only through his encounter with God. It is in God that man finds full self-realization: this is the truth revealed by Christ. Man fulfils himself in God, who comes to meet him through his Eternal Son" (n. 9). This is where the meeting of cultures is really played out. Gedono today is a splendid community of more than thirty sisters. The community's presence in Indonesia has exercised a real fascination also on the Muslim world that surrounds it, which, for all its being far from the Christian faith (and even at times submitting it to persecution), is full of reverence for any genuine experience of prayer to God, Allah, the Most High.

Our Sixth Foundation: Matútum, The Philippines (1995)

Vitorchiano's experience of mission was destined to continue. It did so in obedience to a mandate received, in fidelity to the will of the Church, conscious of its own destiny. This time, the invitation to found was made insistently and movingly from the Order through Dom Joseph Chu Cong, the old and saintly abbot of the monastery of Our Lady of the Philippines on the island of Guimaras.

Our Lady of Matútum takes its name from a volcano on the island of Mindanao. The monastery officially began regular life on 11 June 1995, in a small building intended to become the guesthouse. It had not been easy to find a property that lent itself to the construction of a Cistercian monastery. Given that the immense archipelago of the Philippines is made up of mostly tiny islands accessible only by sea or air, we conducted a complicated search for a terrain that offered not only sufficient space to build a monastery but also possibilities for the development of a line of work that could sustain the community. On the island of Mindanao, one of the largest in the archipelago, it was difficult to find a property with access to water supplies.

Vitorchiano accompanied the birth of this foundation as it had accompanied all the others, although the process was possibly made more difficult on account of the need to use English as a base language and because we experienced the pain of seeing one of the foundresses fall very ill. The enormous distance in terms of both geography and culture called for special effort. Still, the church of Our Lady of Matútum was brought to birth, and Vitorchiano began to familiarize itself with a Divine Office chanted in English while the group of foundresses was formed. Once again, the motherhouse witnessed the departure of people who had enriched the life of the community with their generous service, faithfulness, and competence in various sectors of life and work.

Once the group had arrived in Mindanao, it set about working on community integration, following the same path of purification and effort that all the other foundations had followed. It was far from easy to learn to accept the sisters the way they were, without presuming to change them according to one's own measure; to accept a new superior who had still to learn the patience of motherhood (which is to say, the patience of sacrifice and self-giving) while her own heart keenly longed for the mother she herself had just left behind; to accept the provisional character of circumstances after living in an environment where everything was well organized and provided for; to make space for postulants and novices in quarters that were still narrow and lacking in definition. Yet out of all this, as if by enchantment, a splendid monastery emerged. It is a pure miracle of divine providence that has permitted the community to move into buildings that wonderfully facilitate community life. This monastery will soon be full of the many vocations that already present themselves for the Cistercian life at Matútum. It goes without saying that pain is not lacking. There are instances of poor health to be reckoned with, the effort required to establish a line of work amid considerable difficulties of communication and transport, the threats of distant terrorism and home-grown Islamic fanaticism. Day by day we learn to entrust ourselves to Mystery, to place our trust in the divine will that directed us to this place, following not our own choice but his eternal purpose, so that we may bear witness, here, to his Kingdom.

Within a single year, Vitorchiano saw the departure of ten beloved sisters who went to found in the Philippines while a whole generation of old nuns proceeded to the great foundation in heaven, which for more than a century has gathered the most mature, holiest fruit of our community. The earthly and the heavenly foundation moved together toward the accomplishment of God's will. This fact lets us suppose that Matútum will always be accompanied by holy Vitorchiano nuns whose faithfulness and self-outpouring imbue the old walls of the motherhouse.

Huambo: Valserena's Foundation in Angola

This house, the daughter of a daughter, belongs to the second generation, yet still has its place within the filiation of Vitorchiano. Only Valserena could tell the story of this foundation, which has astonished everyone by being so fruitful, by heroically staying in the breach of an endless war that has ruined a whole nation and people, exposing Huambo to constant, unparalleled danger of reprisal and murder. All the while, countless numbers of poor people were turning up tattered, famished, wounded, and mutilated on the doorstep of the monastery, settled provisionally in an urban dwelling in order to flee the massacre that was spreading like wildfire in the country. Life, however, went on. The people of Huambo have celebrated the solemn professions of these fearless daughters of the Angolan people in their own cathedral.

I remember as if it were yesterday the discussion that took place at the General Chapter of 1987, which elaborated on the various possibilities for a return to their own country of the Angolan sisters then living in the monastery of Santa María de Gratia Dei at Benaguacil in Valencia, Spain. Could they begin to live the Cistercian life in their homeland? Doubt, fear, and perplexity were voiced before such a new, precarious way of making a foundation. The attempt served to show, however, that Angola was a fertile setting thanks to its vitality and thanks to the vocations it produced. It was well able to open up to a youthful, fruitful Cistercian life. The experiment was difficult, troubled, and uncertain. But it led to Valserena's assuming responsibility as life-giver for the Angolan project, given that Benaguacil, at the time, had neither the opportunity nor the required strength to proceed with a foundation. Itself a young foundation, Valserena had to assume a difficult maternity, providing generous assistance to a foundation that was being born on the eve of a massive civil war.

Who can forget the labor of Mother Carla, the bursar of Valserena, who filled and sent off container upon container with indispensable provisions? Who can forget the hours Mother Eugenia spent queuing in food stores to obtain a sack or two of casaba for the community or for the poor; or Mother Geltrude's passion for the poorest, most abandoned people of

Huambo as she commuted through minefields between Lu-
anda and Huambo? Who can forget the fortitude of Mother
Antonia, the community's abbess, or of Sister Emmanuela,
neither of whom ever gave in before the raging of war, ma-
laria, threats, and famine? These silent heroes of Valserena
prepared the ground for the wonderful fruitfulness and fidelity of the Angolan sisters who soon showed themselves to be
a young community full of hardy hope, possessed of the will
to live out their Cistercian monastic vocation. We see in them
a real miracle of life and grace.

Summary

There is something wondrous about this long chronicle of expansion. From it, we could make the following observations:

1. God uses the poorest people to accomplish his works.

2. Genuine fruitfulness is born from obedience to the
   Church. It unfolds within community consensus.

3. It is only by following the path of humility, charity, and
   patience that we can recover and heal situations that are
   ambiguous or vague.

4. Only insofar as we are radically faithful to the tradition,
   charism, and grace received by God through the founding
   house will we succeed in creating something truly new.
   Only then can we embrace inculturation and continuity
   together as the very breath of life with simplicity and in
   truth.

5. The founding house may never abdicate its maternity.
   It must continue to accompany its foundations and give
   them life, even when they have become autonomous. The
   grace from which a monastery is founded must never
   fail. From this generative energy comes the possibility of
   generating further life.

The Path of Sonship

What a long time had to pass
Before I managed to grasp that you do not want
Me to be a father unless at the same time
I am a son.
To receive in oneself the radiance of fatherhood
Does not mean merely "to be a father"
But even more, "to be a child,"
A son.
The more I become a father,
The more I become a child.
— *Karol Wojtyła,* Thoughts on Fatherhood

The path of sonship runs through all the stages of obedience. It is the royal road that leads to the Father. Filial obedience is more than a matter of executing commands. It is an obedience that establishes the entire person within the will of God, to become in all things like the Son who "learned obedience from what he suffered" (Heb 5:8). If by the grace of baptism we are already "sons in the Son," it is by obedience that we enter into the dimension of likeness and conformity to Christ.

Obedience informs the essential relation between the Son and the Father. It is within this trinitarian relation that man is brought to life. To gain access to the heart of this sonship, man is asked to consent to the life given him, to recognize the gift received and to let that eternal relation, that immortal destiny, be alive in every breath he takes.

141

The teaching offered to the novitiate and community of Vitorchiano on the subject of sonship has in these last years been abundant and luminous. In the present chapter, I can do no more than formulate a few reflections on the basis of the riches thus received.

The Theology of Sonship

In speaking about sonship, I intend to speak about following Christ. This following unequivocally requires us to recognize creation as the original fact of our existence. It likewise requires us to cling to the incarnation by which the Son of God became Son of man. It is, then, only through faith that the experience of sonship is opened up to us.

When we accept the reality of the incarnation in the reality of our own lives, we already see something of the Father's glory. We already contemplate his face. We can see his glory if we in turn let ourselves become sons by the Father's gift. This becoming sons corresponds to the form of our being, yet it does not occur unless we choose it. Saint John does not speak of a power to *be* but a power to *become* sons of God (John 1:12). We are destined to become, little by little, sons in the Son. We are destined, that is, to be born from the Spirit and to become adult in faith, and so to attain to the fullness of sonship. The one and true "power" we possess is this: to become sons. In order to hold on to this power, the wellspring of grace for man, we must never abandon the sacred gift of *childhood*, by which I mean the capacity to remain turned toward another, toward the Father, to receive from him constantly his life-giving breath. Only the Son knows the Father. Only the Son receives everything from the Father. Only the Son sees and understands everything in the Father.

We have said that sonship is a dimension of existence that rests wholly on the mystery of creation and incarnation. By situating the notion thus in a setting of faith, we liberate it from interpretations that are sentimental and ambiguous.

We cannot permit ourselves to adopt a childish attitude. We cannot give in to a senseless infantilism that seeks only protection and the satisfaction of need. No! Sonship is an article of faith. It presupposes a radical following of Christ. It involves keeping our eyes fixed on the Father in order to receive life from him. This is a fundamental issue of Christian identity.

The more man forgets where he comes from, the more his life will lose this dimension of mystery. The temptation will be to define life exclusively in terms of categories drawn from science, psychology, or sociology. Our fundamental sin is this: we forget that we exist because we were *wanted*; at the same time, we have the presumption to think of ourselves as our own creators. To live and behave as a mercenary, to operate in a calculating way according to convenience and circumstances, is easier than to live as sons in the supreme freedom of dependence. We lose our substance as persons when we forget about our origin and are unable to receive ourselves as a gift to ourselves, continually given by the Father in the Son.

The loss of memory of our own origin amounts to a loss of identity. When a man underrates the dimension of sonship, therefore, he knows neither who he is, nor where he comes from, nor where he is going. He loses the bearings of his destiny and of the truth of his being. Faith is precisely the recognition that every human being comes from afar and is going even further, beyond temporal existence, beyond the space of immediacy, moving continually toward true birth, toward eternal sonship. We can live fully only if we discover in ourselves the voice of the Spirit that makes us repeat, "Yes, Father, you wanted me!"

In this yes our whole person is engaged. Here we recover the essence of our birth, the core of the mystery of our existence, our true identity. Don Giussani once remarked that "in today's youth, it is as if birth were not a factor to be reckoned with. It is as if the young had not yet reached the awareness of being dependent, the awareness, that is, of having been *wanted*, the feeling of having been *wanted*. This, indeed, is of

supreme importance: the feeling of being *wanted*."[1] The theological basis for the notion of sonship thus rests,

- on a recognition of my own origin, the feeling of having
  been wanted from eternity;

- on the humility I need in order to receive myself from Another, that is, from God and from the people God places
  on my path to guide me with authority toward life and
  growth: the Church, the community, my superior;

- on the experience of freedom as dependence: a freedom
  that accepts the fact of being born and commits itself to
  growth, certain of having an origin and following its destiny, following the Other from whom I receive myself as
  gift;

- on the awareness that only sonship can determine my
  own identity.

Of this we find authoritative confirmation in the *Catechism of
the Catholic Church* when it expounds the meaning of baptism:
"The fruit of Baptism, or baptismal grace, is a rich reality that
includes forgiveness of original sin and all personal sins, birth
into the new life by which man becomes an adoptive son of
the Father, a member of Christ and a temple of the Holy Spirit.
By this very fact the person baptized is incorporated into the
Church, the Body of Christ, and made a sharer in the priest-
hood of Christ" (*CCC* 1279).

The Pedagogy of Sonship

The pedagogy of sonship is fundamentally played out at the
level of obedience. I mean the Gospel obedience born of faith,
which is so much more than merely doing what one is told,
than the docility of perfectionists, than an attitude of accom-
modating passivity. People who are obedient on Gospel terms
generously face the pain of their becoming. They assume re-

sponsibility for their own freedom. The witness of the self-sacrificing love of Christ, "obedient unto death, the death of the Cross" (Phil 2:8), is the great paschal proclamation of the supreme, filial obedience of Christ that is the source of all freedom, that vanquishes fear and human perplexity before pain and death.

Contemporary culture is marked by the evasion of pain. The absence of a "why" before the mystery of life and death, a natural rebellion when faced with suffering, makes man want to anaesthetize existence with painkillers. He *abstracts* reality, seeking refuge in all kinds of pseudo-mysticism, searching for compensation in sublimation and facile emotional excitement.

The true victory over death, meanwhile, is wrought by obedience. Obedience means the eruption of Christ's rising in us, the exultation of dawn shining on the empty tomb of him who was obedient to the point of crucifixion and who leapt from the tomb to eternal life. When we obey, we let our weight of sin and negativity sink into the death of Christ. It thus reemerges from the night of disobedience into the obedient splendor of resurrection.

On the path of sonship, therefore, obedience is put forward not only as liberation but as resurrection and finally as transfiguration, that is, the transformation of a human being into that listening space where alone echoes the Father's voice over Tabor: "This is my beloved Son in whom I am well pleased" (Matt 17:5). Indeed, through being freed from self-will, the new man comes into light. He is clothed with resurrection, reclothed with the victory over death, the victory, in other words, over ontological rebellion: over the illusion of self-sufficiency, over his failure to recognize his origin and destiny. On the Cross, Christ redeems this failure. He gives us, in his blood outpoured, the new *form* of redeemed man, of the One on whom good pleasure rests. Thus, a dimension of transfiguration breaks creaturely limitations open, filling time, space, and history with the eternal recognition of divine sonship: "This is my beloved son in whom I am well pleased."

I have placed the present section under the heading "peda-gogy" precisely because a true model of formation is at stake. It is a matter of learning obedience not on the basis of re-pression, disciplines, and norms but rather on the basis of an awareness of our own identity as sons in the transfigured, risen Son. It is a matter of teaching our young women to be-come daughters, not "good girls"; to launch themselves into life as people who, feeling loved and wanted by the Father, look constantly toward his face and so, in the Father's face, learn to look with abandon and confidence at the face of her who has authority to guide them. The point is not to reproduce the features of that face in a mechanical way but to receive the life-giving guidance they need in order to walk in the truth about themselves. This is the sonship that saves and frees us from the lie of our false autonomies.

Disobedience and the evasion of pain coincide. They are the obvious symptoms of a humanity that considers flight from sonship to be freedom. Filial obedience can only be born of self-sacrificing love, the "dying love" so dear to Hans Urs von Balthasar. We shall know it only if our gaze is always fixed on the Father, to receive from him guidance to live, strength to exist, sense for today, significance for tomorrow. Such a gaze depends on a sense of sonship. It receives everything from this sense. It is permeated by it. People who turn away from this gaze will struggle to find reasons to go on living. Their existence is fragmented into pointless instants, sinking into the anguish of nothingness. They are enslaved to the human self-sufficiency that rises, troubling and suffocating, out of the chaos of pride. We seek to evade pain, yet the absence of a Father in whom to place our trust causes us to sink into the fear of death.

It follows that pain must be faced as an integral part of truly coming to life. Speaking of "Man without Measure," Hans Urs von Balthasar cites H. Rolf to illustrate how authentic love is always bound to death: "Whoever is struck by love, with whatever consequences, experiences love right from the outset as death; it is determined by death and wrested from death, lasts irrevocably until death and leads to death. Love is deadly, because it so changes the love-struck person that he dies to his old life."[2] Once we have been touched by love, we die to ourselves, to our past, to our claims on life. We live only for the one who loves us. To die to self involves pain. Let us not deceive ourselves about this, and let us not try to deceive anyone else. "Today you will be with me in paradise" (Luke 23:43). From where was this great promise given, the promise that cancels out the blasphemous sin of human pride? It was given from the Cross.

We should never tire of repeating and affirming this fundamental educational model, which epitomizes the monastic formation within which it has been given our community to live. It presents obedience as an expression of sonship. Such obedience always presupposes responsible freedom. It is never proud autonomy. It constitutes a space of listening and relationship that accepts pain as a passage to new life and a point of access to transfiguration. The Constitutions of our Order describes the obedience of the monk in the following terms: "In [. . .] renouncing his own will he follows the example of Christ who was obedient until death and commits himself to the school of the Lord's service" (n. 11).

During the Synod of Consecrated Life, many speakers repeated that an obedience that conforms us to God's will is the most eloquent sign of love and holiness, in other words, of perfect charity.[3] The Constitution just cited indicates that the process of renouncing one's own will in order to hand oneself over to the school of the Lord's service represents a single movement of human freedom. I receive myself in order to give myself. I renounce myself in order to hand myself over. This calls for ascesis. I must face the effort it takes to transcend instinctive selfishness and thus the experience of pain, which remains integral to the pedagogy of sonship.

The Ascesis of Sonship

The point of departure for the ascesis of sonship is poverty
of heart. Only people whose hearts are poor know how to
receive the gift of life, know how to receive and maintain, *as
sonship*, the great good of being alive. They find freedom as
they run along the path of humiliation and expropriation.
At Vitorchiano, we have recently developed one of the most
interesting aspects of the ascesis of sonship. The accent has
been placed on the *power* of sonship (*cf.* John 1:12) as the only
possible source of dignity and authority for the human person.
It stands for:

- a power that strips away accretions in order to make us
  put on God;

- a power that serves, since only one who serves possesses
  true authority;

- a power that expropriates, since it affirms only the will
  of the Father and the primacy of our brother;

- a power that purifies, since it accepts the pain of humiliation and limitation, without seeking to evade the pain of
  coming to new life, of clinging to a dynamic of growth;

- a power that sanctifies, since what is born of sonship par-
  takes, in the Son, of God's holiness, and holiness is the
  heritage of the sons of God;

- a power, finally, that acquires substance in obedience, that
  is nourished by dependence, strengthened by humiliation
  and given density by sonship, since without obedience,
  the truth will never become flesh of our flesh.

The ascesis of sonship further follows a progression specific
to itself, through certain stages that lead toward a fullness
of meaning. In this regard I can only repeat what has been
handed on to me.

Renouncing Self-Sufficiency

By this means we put ourselves fully at God's disposal. We overcome the difficulties of life by entrusting ourselves to God who asks and who knows what he is asking for, without envisaging a success rate on the basis of our own possibilities and natural gifts. It is never impossible to obey. When this does seem to be the case, a great opportunity arises for the conversion of our heart and mind to the infinite possibility of God. Insofar as we place ourselves at God's disposal, we become a space in which divine omnipotence can move.

The Option for Gentleness

Obedience wells forth from a gentle heart, a heart that shows its loyalty without contesting and protesting, without polemics, and without wasting time in a loss of confidence. By not wasting time in a loss of confidence, it is able to criticize in a way that is constructive. It develops an instinct for reform. A lowly heart hands itself over to obedience as to the only space in which realism and life can be found.

Openness of Heart

This must obtain with regard to both my abbot and my community. A closed heart is an arrogant heart. Therefore it is given to contradiction. It refuses dialogue, never questions itself, is inaccessible to the word that might effect its conversion, and refuses to accept the sweet yoke of obedience. When we are open of heart, we let go of what is our own. Thereby we confess the sin of our secret ambition, while professing the saving mercy of God.

The Positive Attitude of Humility

This overcomes the negativity inherent in our defensiveness, our irony, and our too reasonable justifications. It helps us to cling to the truth in order to abide in reality. By discovering and accepting our poverty in this way, we touch the creative seal of divine sonship at a very deep level.

Reconciliation and Pardon

These are qualities that can define interpersonal relationships. Someone who is truly a *son* has eyes to see his brother and does not relate to him in a competitive way but with a will to tenderness, pardon, and understanding. He will always risk a gesture of compassion. He will be disposed to giving boundless credit.

Being Ready, Swift, Joyful

At stake here is the immense vitality of Benedictine obedience, which engages the entire life of the monk in a dynamic movement that does away with hesitation, treads fear underfoot, and lets love spring forth. Sonship vanquishes spiritual inertia, *acedia*, that great enemy of love. It is our lack of faith, our inability to believe in the greatness of the eternal vocation given us, that gives rise to *acedia*. Once love fails, hesitations, rationalizations, calculations, and confrontations reign alongside indolence and rejection. To begin to obey is to begin to love and to run, as the Rule has it, on the way of the Lord's commandments (Prol. 49).

In this outline of the ascesis of sonship, we have understood sonship to mean the defeat of the temptation to omnipotence that is ingrained in every human being. We have indicated a deliberate choice of gentleness and lowliness, an openness of heart that goes beyond self-justification, inertia, or flight, as we cling to what is real and practice forgiveness and compassion. It is a model that does not call for a commentary. It needs to be followed, rather, for it is only by investing ourselves in it that we shall be able to pass it on to others.

Sonship and the Church

When we follow Christ, the Son of the Father's good pleasure, we are never on our own. Our following is always an ecclesial event, a source of communion in giving and receiving.

A monastic community has little indeed to give the moment it no longer witnesses to the singular covenant between men that is built on the forgiveness and mercy we have received from the Father in the Son and that, from age to age, weaves the fabric of human history. When the dimension of sonship breaks down in a community, it will soon be up against inevitable generational conflicts and a loss of identity. The common life will seem an enormous effort.

As it happens, Christian conversion itself is never only the fruit of an individual's decision. Conversion has a sacramental structure. It does not designate a private mystical experience but defines the essence of baptism. We are dealing with an ecclesial, sacramental event. By the very mystery of baptism, conversion entails an entrusting of oneself to a *form* impressed by the Holy Spirit.

How does the Holy Spirit work? It works by teaching and calling to mind, by teaching us to listen. Memory digs deep in us and lets us discover that we belong to our origin. Listening, meanwhile, quickens a sense of belonging to the Word in the here and now. We can entrust ourselves to the *form* only in the place where he who became flesh remains flesh, that is, in the Church. In the Church, past and present, subject and object meet. In her, we live as Christ's contemporaries.

How do we see what I have just said reflected in the Cistercian monastic experience? The two fundamental characteristics of the Benedictine coenobium are obedience and belonging. There is a close relationship between obedience and stability, following and belonging. To obey is to remain fixed within God's will, belonging to the concrete space in which the will of God for me is made manifest. The gyrovague is for Saint Benedict someone who does not want to remain settled within this will of God but instead prefers evasion, flight, and roaming, as he "indulges his own will and succumbs to the allurements of gluttony" (RB 1.10f.). Even if he remains physically within the bounds of his own monastery, he does not run the risk posed by belonging but keeps on roaming, filling the void of his heart with the void of stuff.

The Fathers taught that "no one can have God as his Father who does not have the Church as his Mother."[4] It is not from a piecemeal Christ that we receive life but from the whole Christ, head and members, from Christ and the Church. From the beginning of our existence we are surrounded by a love so great, by a mercy so infinite, by a mystery of salvation and forgiveness so amazing that we cannot not open ourselves to passionate love for the Body of the Lord, the Church, from which we continually receive life. The same holds for the community that every day gives us life. To belong is to live out this overflowing love, this embrace that serves and trusts. We truly belong when we reap the mystery of grace of our own community and let it fill our hearts.

When we profess the monastic vow of stability, we profess just this kind of belonging. And profession in turn makes our belonging more profound. Here, sonship appears as a readiness to leave everything for the sake of discipleship, a readiness to embrace all to become the member of a body. The monk is defined by his belonging. He has entrusted himself to each member of his community. Each member of the community has become his own body. We make our belonging visible and concrete, while letting our sonship become manifest, when we obey not only the abbot but every brother. I truly belong when I find myself in my own community.

When a monk's relationship with his community is determined by belonging, he finds himself in the brethren. Looking at the reality of his community, such a monk recognizes himself and says, "This is I." He recognizes himself in the community's history, charism, tradition, and shared vision.

Recognizing himself thus, he can say to each brother: "You are I. And your life is mine."

The Enemies of Sonship

The enemies of sonship spring from *acedia*, the spiritual inertia of which we spoke earlier. According to Evagrius Ponticus and John Cassian, the most common enemies are three in number: aversion to the place, aversion to time, and aversion to the brethren.

Aversion to the Place

A monk who does not live on the basis of sonship is always in search of *another place* to get away from the pain and difficulty of remaining. The recurring note is the claim that the space in which he presently lives is inadequate for one reason or another, that it does not nurture the spiritual life but rather is an obstacle to it. If the soul in its depths harbors sadness (and what greater sadness is there than that of not feeling a son?), the soul will constantly try to get away from itself and hence from the place of its belonging: "Man is afraid to be alone with himself, he loses his centre and becomes a mental and spiritual vagabond who is always out. The symptoms of this footloose restlessness are garrulousness [*verbositas*] and inquisitiveness: from thought man runs away into talking; since he has lost the vision of eternity he is launched on an insatiable search for surrogates."[5]

Aversion to Time

Time is no longer perceived as favorable time, a time of consequence in which God speaks to me and addresses me. Apart from our relationship with God, there cannot be a favorable time. Cut off from transcendence, time no longer makes sense, whether as present or future. Only sonship bestows on time the density of an occasion, confers on the present moment the grace to perceive an infinite Presence.

Aversion to the Brethren

Finally, the disgust and sadness of the heart are projected onto others. There is no forgiveness for the past, no compassion for the present. What remains is resentment, discontent, and even sometimes vindictiveness. Sonship is principally endangered when we forget where we come from and who we are, our origin and our destiny. We then start living on the surface of existence, prey to the arrogant illusion of self-sufficiency.

These brief notes on the path to follow toward sonship indicate the principal lines for a pedagogy of belonging. I am conscious that what I have said is partial and fragmentary. At the same time I wish to express my gratitude for the rich teaching that has been so generously given us.

> *They will take Your hands*
> *away from my arms—Son, can You see*
> *this annihilation—when the day comes*
> *I will give Your bright light*
> *to the corn on the swelling earth.*
>
> *Father, my hands lost from Your arms*
> *I will weld to a tree*
> *stripped of its green,*
> *and with the pale light of wheat*
> *fill this great brightness*
> *that You change into ears of corn.*

> —*Karol Wojtyła*, Song of a Hidden God[6]

Epilogue

On Prayer

When our heart prays, it breathes. Prayer makes us joyful, strong, and courageous. Prayer makes our heart beat and provides oxygen for our whole body. Prayer irrigates our being. Perhaps we are here putting our finger on the cause of so much sullenness in the Church and in society: the fact that the practice of prayer has reached a very low level. When that happens, the heart is weighed down by a dead weight. A Church that does not pray is like a batch of dough that has collapsed. No other leaven can raise it from its apathy. The Spirit prays in us. Surrounded by chatter, it whispers "with sighs too deep for words" (Rom 8:26).

—*Cardinal Godfried Daneels*, The Consoler[1]

In a text that sets out to propose a monastic pedagogy, it seems necessary to say something about an introduction to prayer or methods of prayer. But is there method in prayer? We all yearn for prayer. It is quite true that prayer is like "the breathing of our heart that gives oxygen to the whole body." Pure prayer, meanwhile, is a gift of the Spirit, a gift for the few, perhaps, though nonetheless a gift for all. It is what any seeker after God dreams of with infinite longing. To translate the longing in descriptive, experiential terms is like trying to explain the working of the profound "breathing" that transcends human feeling absolutely. And who ever could do such a thing?

Perhaps it will be possible, though, for me to speak humbly of a few concrete facts that have remained in my remembrance of my own life, facts that represent indelible impressions of

155

a mysterious perception of that divine Beyond to which true prayer carries us.

Could I have been three years old? My parish showed special fervor in its celebration, in August, of the annual novena to Nostra Signora della Guardia, Our Lady of Refuge, who was the diocese's patron. Her sanctuary towered over our city of Genoa as the destination of continuous pilgrimages. When these novenas took place, normally at about eight o'clock in the evening, a famous preacher was invited, the faithful filled the church, and the great painting of Our Lady of Refuge was given a place of honor next to the presbytery. The organ thundered the popular Marian hymns we all knew and sang at the top of our voices: "I shall go to see her one day, in heaven, my homeland!" What fascinated my childish imagination more than anything else were the lights, all of which were lit. An infinite number of chandeliers gleamed from all the arches of the church. Not a single corner was left in darkness. Before the large Marian image there was a profusion of flowers, every bit as resplendent as a living fountain of light. My family was poor. We still had only petroleum lamps. This profusion of light and flowers, combined with the singing, therefore filled my heart with amazement. My childish heart always asked itself if this was not in fact paradise? Naturally I did not understand much, perhaps only the fact that it was the feast of Our Lady, and therefore the feast of us all. I invariably fell asleep during the sermon, but my sleep too was full of light, song, and flowers, indelibly impressed on the retina of my heart. My poor mother had to carry me home in her arms, for I was never able to wake up once I had fallen asleep. I remember, though, that my first thought on awakening in the morning was always the same: "*Mamma*! When are we going to the novena?"

Over the years the celebrations took on more modest dimensions, while it took just a couple of bombs to blow up the entire parish in the war of 1940–1944. No weight of circumstances, however, could ever deprive my heart of the sheer feast of the novena, of the infinite security of a child that falls asleep in its mother's arms while the people are singing, "I shall go to see her one day!"

Was this prayer? Perhaps it was more than prayer. It was an experience of paradise beginning on earth, the certainty of being immersed in the feast of faith, the abandonment of someone who moves through the night of this life in the arms of a mother who will never let you fall into the void of the abyss. Perhaps no other experience of prayer can ever quite match this wonderful overlap of the Church and paradise, of my earthly mother and my heavenly Mother.

At five, I made my First Communion. I have very clear memories of the First Communion party. Even more clearly, however, I remember how we were first being tested in the catechism, and how there was tremendous excitement because it was the archbishop who came to examine us. He would, we were told, distribute medals that corresponded to the prompt-ness of our answers. I was awarded a gold medal, and for years I was convinced that this gold represented the ultimate of the eighteen carats our world can provide. Only much later did I come to know that it was only a bit of gilded tin. My surprise was great and painful. At five, though, the medal had been as brilliant as gold, as fine as the finest gold in the world. And so my memory retained the extreme importance of knowing one's catechism really well.

Was it prayer to repeat by rote that God is great, infinitely good, omnipotent, omniscient, omnipresent; to memorize the Creed and the Acts of Faith, Hope, and Love? Perhaps it was not prayer. Still, it was a way of letting faith shape my memory and my heart.

A second memory related to First Communion concerns the feast of Corpus Christi, one week later. All the girls who had been among the communicants got to wear their white dress again, and the smallest among us were positioned, with small baskets of rose petals around our necks, just before the baldachin under which the parish priest solemnly carried the monstrance. It was our task to throw our petals up toward the monstrance all along the procession like sweet incense. As we proceeded, a carpet of petals was formed. During those moments I felt attracted to the shining monstrance. I could not contain my joy when one of the many rose petals we threw by the handful came to touch it. Such was my enthusiasm that I did not interrupt the shower of rose petals for a single moment. And so I wept with total despair once my basket was empty. My mother had to take me out of the procession because of my uncontrollable weeping. At that moment, it was the very height of childish despair to have run out of flowers to throw toward the Lord as he passed through our streets and under the arches of our church. At five years of age, we are still very innocent. We identify ourselves totally with what we are doing, as if our action were our breath of life. I have often asked myself whether prayer is not, in fact, just such an attitude of risking everything for the sake of all-consuming adoration, rejecting all thought of gain, all half-measures, being seized by a Presence, by the explosive desire that one of my poor, half-penny rose petals should touch the divine. Even today, if I close my eyes, I can see myself reaching into my poor little basket for a few fading petals in order to throw them at the Other, throwing them *all*. And I pray that in the concave space of the heart this gesture of daily poverty will continue, that I will never cease risking all to see the petals of my days fall slowly in adoration toward the Presence that fills my life.

I had barely turned eleven when my mother died. The day before I had been playing on my mother's large bed in the hospital ward. She pretended to be dead while I prepared her body, folding her hands and giving her a flower to hold. I was not pleased with the arrangement, and so instead crossed her arms on her breast and twined a rosary through her fingers. I then turned to the flowers, which I arranged in her beautiful black hair. I ordered her to close her eyes and not to move while I started singing the songs I liked best, such as *Volare, oh oh!* My mother let me carry on and took part in the game, although twenty-four hours later she was to be carried off by the high fever of violent meningitis. Later, I was taken to see her in the mortuary, but I found the immobile, waxen figure entirely alien. I hated the people who showed me compassion because of the misfortune that had struck me.

Death for me was not the spectacle of the mortuary. It was the serene play we had shared, with infinite intimacy and tenderness, to prepare a beloved being for tranquil sleep so that her awakening should take place in the sweetness of abandonment, in the spousal peace of a beauty that, at thirty-nine years of age, was at its most resplendent. I never thought of my mother's death as something final. I thought of it as a passage to another world, in which she remains intensely alive, adorned with the last flower I had placed in her raven-black hair, waiting to resume with me the splendid play of living. And all was prayer. For prayer is nothing other than this abandonment to a Beyond that carries us across time, clothed with the eternal youth of God, which from eternity prepares for us a place in his eternal day.

As an adolescent I was troubled, disorderly, and rebellious. My one luminous refuge was the unnoticed corner of a church I would seek out to plan difficult essays or to prepare my hardest exams. I had no idea what prayer was, but it was only within a church, conscious of a Presence in the tabernacle whose flickering sanctuary lamp I could just glimpse, that I was able to study without my memory collapsing into a cloud of vague notions. Only there could I write an essay. Only there could I formulate a thought without being carried by distraction into the most absurd meanderings. Some people were scandalized by my odd place of refuge. Others mocked me for it. But my ability to think, create, and memorize was given me by Another; of this I was well aware. This was a space I shared with God. What was to remain with me was the awareness, a bit confused of course, and tinged with romance, that anything we are given to do comes to us from Another.

Then, if my teachers at school asked me, "Did you really write this? It does not seem like your work!" they were quite right. Within my limitations, Another had been at work, bringing the task to completion. In this way I learned that to pray is to believe in the Spirit's indwelling presence. I learned that what brings accomplishment to our lives is not our human effort, but the eternal counsel of the Holy of Holies.

There followed a time of growth, of enthusiastic membership of a youth group, of great passion for the Church. I was formed as a person and learned more about my faith. I developed a new and intense sense of friendship. I was hungry to live for something worthwhile. I learned a kind of prayer that consisted of self-forgetfulness, of passion for an ideal, of joy in serving the Church. At that time we were carried away by a sense of ourselves as the people of God "in the firing line." Was it euphoria? Quite possibly.

Already, however, my path of faith was shaped by grief. When I was twenty-six years old my best friend, Agnese Simoni, died. She was only twenty-three. Something of me died with her. A few months before she died, Agnese wrote me the following in a letter:

> While you were climbing the Piz Boé, I stayed behind in the cottage, watching the summit toward which you were bound. It was clear to me that I would no longer be able to run along with you toward snow-clad peaks and dizzying heights, those amazing mountains that gave such remarkable zest to our youth. It was clear to me that I had, now, other peaks to reach. And within me a peace of acceptance was born that carried the same splendor as the mountaintops of the Pordoi Pass.

From Agnese Simoni came the yes to death, the supreme yes to God's will, a yes lived out in a friendship so warm that it already had a taste of heaven. How do we pray in the face of death? "I know that nothing of the beauty of this life will ever be taken from me, not even the loveliest corners of this

my plain of Polesine, with its slow procession of poplars that
contemplate their mirror image in the canals. Nothing! Not
even the fragrance of the strawberries you have just given
me." In the face of death we learn the supreme prayer that
consists in the acceptance of mystery, of a destiny, of a cross
that carries us into eternity.

After this came my encounter with the monastery. It was
an encounter marked by contradiction and fascination, dominated by the singular, indecipherable feeling of having at last
come home. My relationship with God was here immersed into
the reality of the Church at prayer. It was an immersion into
deep waters, where faith flows in the great river of psalmody,
where hope rises before dawn, filling the night with remembrance. When I had just entered as a postulant, the novice
mistress sometimes instructed us not to rise for Vigils. I myself
tended to lose track of time, and would sometimes find myself
in the dark cloister in which the first rays of morning light
suggested the outlines of the arches while from the church I
could hear the waves of Gregorian psalmody, as if it came ooz-
ing out of the very walls. Such moments resounded with the
infinite dialogue between God and humankind. Time seemed
to have been suspended. It has never since been granted me
to relive that dazed perception of the night illumined by faith
through the slow transmutation of dawn while the music of
space expressed itself in prayer through silence.

I understood then that everything could be plunged into
this deep sea of endless praise, notwithstanding my poverty,
my distractions, the fragility of the imagination, and the weariness of the body. I saw how everything belongs within the
remembrance of favors received. From Abraham until today,
this remembrance never ceases to amaze creation. It finds
daily, condensed expression in the sacrament of the altar. The
liturgy became the air I breathed.

I do not think I have ever understood a great deal about
chant. About liturgical disquisitions, I understand still less.
Yet into the river of the liturgy that carries humanity toward

the sea of trinitarian Being—yes, into these deep waters my life was plunged as into absolute joy. When on the occasion of great feasts Vigils went on for hours on end, taking off in the stupendous modulations of Gregorian responsories, I always asked myself if this would not happen to be, in fact, ecstasy? It was not. Was it prayer? I am not quite certain, but it was certainly a recognizing oneself in the Baptist's experience of old: "I am the voice of one who calls out in the desert." At night, this voice sings our waiting for the light of dawn. It sings at midday, resonant with heat and fatigue. It sings in the evening, when a longing arises to be consumed and to flourish eternally in the bosom of the Father. It sings at nightfall, calling for true rest and abandoning itself, in the *Salve*, to the Mother of Heaven. I do not know whether this was prayer. It was the form that gave definition to our life. It was the breath of our being through the passing of time. Above all, it was thankfulness, causing us to exclaim, with the wonder of Saint Francis: "Why is this given to me? Why to me? Why to me?"

Later I learned from the living and dying of our old sisters how prayer is embodied in life. I remember Mother Sebastiana, one of the foundresses of Hinojo. She was forty years old, one of the ablest, strongest people I have ever known, a giant of six foot one with the boundless heart of a child. Cancer carried her off in a short time, and in her last days, past and future were for her merged in a single present. It was impressive to hear her speak of Vitorchiano, the place from which she had come, in a way that was at once limpid and confused. Sebastiana always referred to it as "my Jerusalem" and instinctively saw its beauty, vitality, and fruitfulness. She prophesied its history. She drew its features. We thought spontaneously of that mysterious force of prayer that was being carried to fulfillment in the amazing crumbling of the thin wall that divides heaven and earth, time and eternity, the Jerusalem of paradise and that of our earthly pilgrimage. Is prayer, then, this simultaneous transposition of heaven to earth and of earth to heaven? The death of Sebastiana unraveled for us this mystery's significance.

The same could be said for the death of Mother Scholastica, an old lay sister who had spent her entire life working in the orchard. We loved her and we felt compassion for her limitations, for the fragile equilibrium of her mind and the heaviness of her body. Hers was a human poverty resplendently oriented by obedience. Mother Scholastica loved to obey. It filled her with great satisfaction and pride to receive an order from the abbess. The rosary was perhaps the only prayer that her poor mind could really remember properly. She recited it in a manner quite her own, with moving fidelity. "To these little ones does the kingdom of heaven belong." One lovely summer evening the community had gone down to choir after gathering round the bed of Mother Scholastica, who was dying. Two nuns were always left to pray in her sick room, and I was there, contemplating the dying woman's face. A great silence descended. Through the window we could hear the chanting of psalmody, a melody of prayer that filled the room with peace. Suddenly, just as the *Magnificat* was intoned, it was as if the door opened gently and someone entered, invisible to the eyes of the flesh, but quite obvious to the eyes of the spirit. Mother Scholastica's face assumed an expression of great peace and two pure, humble tears fell from her half-closed eyes. That was all. There was not a stir, not a shudder, not a sigh. Mother Scholastica had gone to heaven in the company of the one who had entered, while the chanting of the *Magnificat* filled the infirmary room with a Marian presence. No one could doubt that an encounter had taken place in this serene passing. No one could doubt that Mother Scholastica's "*Mamma* in heaven" had come to take her poor daughter by the hand to guide her gently across the threshold of this temporal life. No one could doubt it. And see, this is prayer: someone comes and takes you by the hand to lead you toward a definitive, wonderful encounter, someone to whom you cannot but abandon yourself in the endless thanksgiving of a life utterly given.

I have discovered, then, that abandonment and thankfulness are the two essential components of prayer and that prayer can only be defined as an encounter with the Lord of life:

> All our activity, our joy and happiness, our work, our life's anxiety should be nothing other than a passionate effort to understand, feel and desire ever more this personal relationship with infinite Love. Our sadness is this: that we cannot see, feel, and touch this relationship after the manner of things here below. Therefore it too often happens that symbols try to get the better of us, quenching in earthly mist the life force that would raise us on wings of passion to the Father's embrace.[2]

Conclusion

Can we append a conclusion to our search for a monastic pedagogy? Any pedagogy consists of continual searching, continual development as it strives to accompany men and women in their history, in their becoming. The subject of this book has been the slow growth of a particular community. We would like to pass on our experience to new generations, who will continue to elaborate the heritage in fidelity to the vocation they have received. A charism is never a static reality. It is something living and dynamic. For what we have been given thus far, we are grateful to God. As we continue to labor today, it is wonderful to draw from an ancient wellspring that has slaked the thirst of many a generation that has gone before us. It continues to flow for others still to come.

In 1965, when the last nun of San Vito, Mother Teresa Bottasso, died, just then, and quite unexpectedly, there arrived at Vitorchiano the large wooden crucifix that had dominated the small chapel of San Vito from above the altar. It was at San Vito that our community was given life in 1875. To receive that cross was to learn a valuable lesson. From age to age, it is the Lord Jesus, and he alone, who is passed on as the heart and soul of the monastic vocation, as the sole source of life and meaning. Or rather, he passes himself. He offers himself to every human being with unfailing fidelity. By calling people to the monastic life, he ensures that the charism of total dedication to him remains alive. Our pedagogy is grafted onto this transmission. It is constantly imbued with new life. Its perspectives, both in seeking and in seeing, become ever vaster.

Thus it helps us to remain at the heart of the vocation we have received. A story from the *Lausiac History* of Palladius may be allowed to bring our reflections to an end:

> There was a certain Paul, a rustic herdsman, simple and entirely without guile, who was married to a most beautiful woman of debased character. She kept her faults hidden for the longest possible time. When Paul returned from the field without warning, he found [her and her lover] carrying on shamefully. It was Providence which had shown him the way that was best. He smiled and told them: "Good, all right, it does not matter to me. Jesus help me, I will have nothing more to do with her. Go, have her and her children, too; I am going off to be a monk." Telling no one, he hastened away the distance of eight steps and came to Blessed Antony and knocked at his door. Antony came out and asked him: "What do you want?" He said he wished to be a monk. Antony said: "A man of sixty years, you cannot become a monk here. Go back to your village instead and work, live an active life, giving thanks to God. You would never endure the trials and tribulations of the desert." Again the old man replied: "I will do whatever you teach me." Antony told him: "I have told you that you are an old man and cannot endure this life. However, if you really wish to be a monk, go to a community of brothers who can put up with your weakness. I live here alone, starving myself with five-day fasts." These are the very arguments he used to scare Paul away. Since he was not going to put up with him, Antony closed the door and did not go out for three days, not even when necessary. But Paul did not go away. On the fourth day Antony was compelled to go out. He opened the door and told him once more: "Old man, you must leave this place. Why do you bother me? You cannot remain here." Paul said: "I cannot die anywhere else but here." Antony observed that he had no food and drink with him, and this was now the fourth day of his fasting. He received him, simply because he feared that the man might die and the guilt would be on his soul. At this time Antony had adopted a way of life more severe than he had ever practiced in his younger days. So he moistened palm leaves and told him: "Take these. Weave a

rope as I am doing." The old man wove until the ninth hour, struggling to complete fifteen ells. Antony watched him and was not pleased. "You wove badly," he said. "Unbraid it and begin over." All this distasteful work was imposed on the old man so that he might become irritable and flee from Antony. But he unwove the palm leaves and braided the same ones again, although it was more difficult, because they were wrinkled and dried up. Antony was moved to pity when he noticed that the man did not grumble, or lose heart, or become angry. When the sun had set, he asked him: "Are you willing to eat a piece of bread?" Paul replied: "As seems best to you, Father." And again Antony was stabbed to the quick because he did not jump eagerly at the mention of food but left the decision to the other. He set the table and brought the bread. Antony laid out the biscuits which weighed six ounces and moistened one for himself—for they were dry—and three for him. Then he intoned a psalm which he knew, and when he had sung it twelve times, he prayed twelve times, in order to test Paul. Paul joined him willingly in prayer again, for he preferred, as I believe, to herd scorpions than to live with an unfaithful wife. After the twelve prayers they settled down to eat, it being quite late. Antony ate one of the biscuits but did not partake of a second. But the old man was eating his small biscuit slowly, and Antony waited until he finished and said: "Eat another one, too, Father." Paul replied: "If you eat one, so will I; if you do not, neither will I." Antony said: "I have had enough. I am a monk." "I have had enough, too," said Paul, "for I wish to be a monk also." Antony got up then and prayed twelve prayers and sang twelve psalms. Then he took a little of his first rest, and at midnight he got up again to sing psalms till it was day. As he noticed the old man willingly following his way of life, he said to him: "If you can do this from day to day, stay with me." Paul answered: "If there is anything further, I do not know, but I can readily do what I have seen." The following day Antony said to him: "Behold, you have become a monk."[1]

According to Thomas Merton, this story says something essential about monastic theology. "I could not possibly die

anywhere but here." We are called to live and die at the heart
of the calling God has given us, at the heart of the monastic
community in which he lets us live, at the heart of the Church
to whom our lives belong as secret roots from which she draws
her fecundity. The point of our pedagogy is to accompany this
habit of *abiding*. Through the patient, never-ending labor of
monastic formation, it builds up the monk's heart in fidelity to
grace received. It establishes him as a member of the Church.
It assists his configuration to Christ. For Christ continues from
age to age his work of transfiguration to make of *man* a *son* in
whom the Father is well pleased.

Notes

Introduction—pages xvii–xxxvi

1. "Les 'oublis' de l'histoire officielle. Mémoires et malmémoires," *Le Monde Diplomatique* (August 1997): 3.

2. "Il perdono, un atto di amore gratuito," *La Traccia* 12 (1996): 1550.

3. Cf. Luigi Giussani, "Tu o dell'amicizia," in the supplement to *Tracce* 6 (1997): 14.

4. *La vita come compito. Appunti autobiografici* (Torino: Società Editrice Internazionale, 1997), 93.

5. *La vita come compito*, 44.

6. This image is developed in Baldwin's fourth *Tractatus*.

7. Luigi Giussani, "Il drama di Clemente Rebora," in *Le mie letture* (Milano: Biblioteca Universale Rizzoli, 1985), 57.

8. *An Interrupted Life: The Diaries and Letters of Etty Hillesum 1941–1943*, trans. Arnold J. Pomerans (London: Persephone, 1999), 268f.

9. From a letter dated 20 March 1940, in *Lettere sul dolore* (Milano: Biblioteca Universale Rizzoli, 1995), 61f.

10. Text printed in *La Traccia* 7–8 (1997): 824–26.

11. Letter 76 (73 in the Cistercian edition) to Rainald of Foigny, in *The Letters of St Bernard of Clairvaux*, trans. Bruno Scott James (Stroud: Sutton, 1998), 106.

12. Letter 87 (85 in the Cistercian edition) to William of Saint-Thierry, in *The Letters of St Bernard of Clairvaux*, 126.

13. Letter 1 to Robert, his nephew, in *The Letters of St Bernard of Clairvaux*, 6f.

14. Letter 75 (72 in the Cistercian edition) to Rainald of Foigny, in *The Letters of St Bernard of Clairvaux*, 106.

15. Sermon 69 *De diversis*, in *S. Bernardi Opera*, ed. Jean Leclercq and others, 8 vols. (Rome: Editiones Cistercienses, 1957–72), 6/1:303f.

16. Letter 190 to Pope Innocent, in *S. Bernardi Opera*, 8:38.

Our History—pages 1–15

1. A. Gramsci, *Quaderni XXVIII*, cited by Luigi Giussani, "Natale per dimenticare il nulla," *La Repubblica* (27 December 1997): 15.

2. *Meditation on the "communio personarum*," a conference given at Vitorchiano on 19 August 1995. Typescript in the archives of Vitorchiano.

Learning From History 1—pages 16–27

1. The quotation is from *Exordium Magnum*, 1.13.

2. These notes draw freely on Dom Patrick Olive's article "Dom Jean-Baptiste Chautard 1858–1935: Pour un cinquantenaire," *Collectanea Cisterciensia* 48 (1986): 3–8.

3. Cited by René Bonpain in his article "Il y a 100 ans . . . L'enfant Jésus et Dom Vital Lehodey, abbé (1895) de Bricquebec," *Collectanea Cisterciensia* 57 (1995): 11.

4. "Il y a 100 ans," 24.

5. Thomas Merton, *The Waters of Siloe* (New York: Harcourt, 1949), 192.

6. *The Waters of Siloe*, 192f.

7. Maur Standaert, "Anselme Le Bail," in *Dictionnaire de Spiritualité*, vol. 9 (Paris: Beauchesne, 1976), col. 448.

8. "La Vocation du Père Thomas Merton," *Collectanea Cistercensia* 48 (1986): 9–18.

9. *The Sign of Jonas* (San Diego, New York, London: Harcourt, 1981), 362.

10. *Thoughts in Solitude* (Tunbridge Wells: Burns and Oates, 1993), 37f.

11. "La Vision contemplative de Thomas Merton," *Collectanea Cisterciensia* 40 (1978): 249.

12. *The Sign of Jonas*, 361.

13. *The Asian Journal of Thomas Merton* (New York: New Directions, 1968), 342f.

14. "A Letter on the Contemplative Life," in *The Monastic Journey*, ed. by Patrick Hart (New York: Image Books, 1978), 222–23.

Learning From History 2—pages 28–48

1. Gabriel Sortais, *Les Choses qui plaisent à Dieu* (Bellefontaine: Éditions de Bellefontaine, 1967), 11.

2. *Les Choses qui plaisent*, 67f.

3. *Les Choses qui plaisent*, 33f.

4. *Les Choses qui plaisent*, 376.

5. *Les Choses qui plaisent*, 384.

6. Joseph Ratzinger, *To Look on Christ*, trans. Robert Nowell (Middlegreen, Slough: St Paul Publications, 1991), 68.

7. *To Look on Christ*, 70f.

8. *To Look on Christ*, 76f.

The Vision of the Church—pages 49–63

1. "L'homme par la communauté: La dynamique de la communication," *Supplément de La Vie spirituelle* 22 (1969): 417, 419.

2. Synodus episcoporum, *La vita consacrata e la sua missione nella Chiesa e nel mondo*, 13.10.1994, n. 21.

3. Passage from a talk given at a leadership meeting of the movement Communion and Liberation at La Thuile, 1995. Typescript in the archives of Vitorchiano.

4. *La vita consacrata*, n. 5.

5. Typescript in the archives of Vitorchiano.

6. *La vita consacrata*, n. 14.

The Path of Conversion—pages 64–80

1. Hans Urs von Balthasar, *Theo-Drama: Theological Dramatic Theology*, vol. 2, "The *Dramatis Personae*: Man in God," trans. by Graham Harrison (San Francisco: Ignatius Press, 1990), 242.

2. "Un espace spirituel ecclésial: le monastère bénédictin," *Collectanea Cisterciensia* 43 (1981): 121–22 (citing Emmanuel Mounier, *Le personnalisme* [Paris: Presses Universitaires de France, 1962], 51f.).

3. *Sapienza monastica. Saggi di storia, spiritualità e problemi monastici* (Roma: Studia Anselmiana, 1994), 473ff.

4. *Vita Sancti Malachiae*, 26.57, in *S. Bernardi Opera*, 3:361.

5. "On Conversion, a Sermon to Clerics," 2.3, in Bernard of Clairvaux, *Sermons on Conversion*, trans. Marie-Bernard Saïd (Kalamazoo, MI: Cistercian Publications, 1981), 34.

6. "On Conversion, a Sermon to Clerics," 3.4, in *Sermons on Conversion*, 35.

7. On Conversion, a Sermon to Clerics," 7.12, in *Sermons on Conversion*, 46.

8. *On Grace and Free Choice*, trans. Daniel O'Donovan, CF 19A (Kalamazoo, MI: Cistercian Publications, 1988), 6.18; p. 73f.

9. "Life and Writings of Br. M. Rafael Barón (VII)," *Cistercian Studies Quarterly* 38 (2003): 57f.

10. J. Dobracynski, *Encuentros con la Señora. Historias del Santo Icono de la Virgen de Częstochowa* (Madrid: Palabras, S.A., n.d.), 326.

On Teaching How to Love—pages 81–104

1. Cited in Charles Moeller's *Littérature du XXe siècle et christianisme*, vol. 5, *Amours humaines* (Louvain: Casterman, 1975), 15.

2. From *Dans un mois, dans un an*, cited in *Littérature du XXe siècle et christianisme*, 5:17.

3. *Littérature du XXe siècle et christianisme*, 5:20.

4. From *Les Merveilleux nuages*, cited in *Littérature du XXe siècle et christianisme*, 5:26.

5. *Littérature du XXe siècle et christianisme*, 5:25.

6. *An Interrupted Life*, 249f.

7. *An Interrupted Life*, 242.

8. *An Interrupted Life*, 281.

9. *An Interrupted Life*, 282.

10. *An Interrupted Life*, 259.

11. *An Interrupted Life*, 233.

12. *An Interrupted Life*, 220f.

13. *An Interrupted Life*, 221.

14. Homily for the Mass of the Lord's Supper, 16 April 1981, *La Traccia* 4 (1981) 323.

15. Address to participants in the congress *La famiglia e l'amore*, *La Traccia* 5 (1981): 381.

16. Karol Wojtyła (John Paul II), *Love and Responsibility*, trans. H. T. Willetts (London: Collins, 1981), 166–73.

17. *Love and Responsibility*, 258.

18. Gertrude the Great of Helfta, *The Herald of God's Loving-Kindness*, trans. Alexandra Barratt (Kalamazoo, MI: Cistercian Publications, 1991), 2.3.3; p. 107.

19. *The Herald*, 2.3.4; p. 103f.

20. *The Herald*, 2.21.4; p. 159.

21. *The Herald*, 2.24.2; p. 173.

Monasticism and Mission—pages 105–19

1. Joseph Aubry, *Teologia della vita consacrata*, in *Vita consacrata. Un dono del Signore alla sua Chiesa*, ed. Italian Bishops' Conference (Rivoli: Elledici, 1993), 207–8.

2. "Moine et mission: Réflexions à partir de Vatican II sur la responsabilité missionnaire," *Bulletin de l'A.I.M. pour l'aide et le dialogue* 43 (1987): 11f.

3. "Foundations as Mission in the Life of the Order," *Cistercian Studies Quarterly* 18 (1983): 331.

4. "Foundations as Mission," 333.

5. "Foundations as Mission," 337.

6. "Foundations as Mission," 339.

7. "Maria, aurora della nostra salvezza" (Castelgandolfo, 8 September 1964), in *Encicliche e discorsi di Paolo VI* (Rome: Edizioni Paoline, 1965), 4:33.

Foundations—pages 120–40

1. "Fundaciones en los últimos cincuenta años de la Orden Cisterciense de la Estrecha Observancia," *Cistercium* 194 (1993): 519.

2. "Messaggio alle claustrali dell'America Latina" (29 December 1989), *La Traccia* 12 (1989): 1387–88.

The Path of Sonship—pages 141–54

1. Giovanni Testori and Luigi Giussani, *Il senso della nascita* (Milan: Rizzoli, 1980), 23.

2. *Theo-Drama: Theological Dramatic Theology*, vol. 2, "The *Dramatis Personae*: Man in God," 418 (citing H. Rolf, *Der Tod in der mittelhochdeutschen Dichtung* [Munich: Fink, 1974], 380).

3. Cf. *Vita Consacrata*, nn. 21f. and 91.

4. Cyprian of Carthage, *De catholicae ecclesiae unitate*, 6.

5. Ratzinger, *To Look on Christ*, 72.

6. Trans. Jerzy Peterkiewicz, www.philosophyoffreedom.com/
node/2145; accessed 16 May 2012.

Epilogue: On Prayer—pages 155–64

1. *Le Consolateur: Paroles de vie, Noël 1997* (Mechelen: Service de
Presse de l'Archeveché, 1997), 37.
2. Luigi Giussani, *Lettere di fede e di amicizia* (Milano: San Paolo,
1993), 24.

Conclusion—pages 165–68

1. Palladius, *The Lausiac History*, trans. Robert T. Meyer, Ancient
Christian Writers 34 (Mahwah, NJ: Paulist Press, 1964), 76–79.